MW00943125

Stories from the Hart

Anne Hart Preus

author HOUSE®

AuthorHouse™
1663 Liberty Drive
Bloomington, IN 47403
www.authorhouse.com
Phone: 1-800-839-8640

First published by AuthorHouse 2/25/2011

ISBN: 978-1-4567-2284-5 (e)
ISBN: 978-1-4567-2283-8 (sc)

Library of Congress Control Number: 2011900795

Printed in the United States of America

Dedication

This book is dedicated to my parents, James Hart "Choctaw" and Annie Laurie "Dink" Morrow; to my brothers, Will and Robert Morrow; and to my children, Christian, Anna, and Oliver Preus.

Table of Contents

Preface

Years ago, I started walking early in the morning for exercise and to have a little time to think. Usually, it was the only alone time I had, and those precious minutes afforded me the opportunity to ponder many things and to wonder what may lie ahead for the day or week. I reveled in the fresh air—hot and humid in the summer, and cold, damp, and piercing in the winter. I marveled at the changing seasons and the sounds and smells of each one.

I have continued that practice of walking as my years have advanced, and with every step I am grateful to be outside, to live where I live, and to have experienced such a unique place as the Mississippi Delta, which is and has been home for all of my life.

My children have asked me what it was like growing up in the country (rural Tallahatchie County) in the 1950s and '60s. I never really have given them an answer, partially because I did not care to dredge up long lost memories and partially because I did not think there was anything special to relate. Truthfully, I really did not want to acknowledge the fact that so many years had passed, and I did not want to own up to being in my senior years. Lately, though, as I walk on the turn row running through the rice and cornfields and watch as the sun rises on a new day, observing the magical layers of mists dancing over the fields, I realize that though so many things have changed, they remain the same. The advent of technology changed our world. Social upheavals marked new ways of thinking, of interacting, of boundaries; and war and assassinations made indelible impressions on my generation. The 1960s had many significant events making it stand out in the annals of history. No other decade has thrust so much on a nation or the world.

I am fortunate to have had the experience of growing up in that time. My children cannot comprehend what life was like without Internet, microwaves, television, or (horrors, forbid) cell phones. So I have attempted to compile scenarios of those years for historical or perhaps hysterical purposes. The characters and events have not been changed to protect the innocent because we were all innocent then. It was a time when nobody locked a door, and we felt safe. In truth, we were insulated from some of the harsh realities and the changes taking place in the world. Our world was a small portion of Tallahatchie County, and we knew only of that place. The people that entered and exited our lives created indelible impressions and left a part of themselves with us. These stories represent a time and place that will always exist in our memories. For some, the memories may be painful. For others, they are a chance to reminisce about people and things long forgotten. For still others, they will realize that the more things have changed, the more they have stayed the same. Connections, family, church, and school have bound us together with everlasting ties. This book is written for those who grew up in the middle decades of the twentieth century and for their children and grandchildren who wonder what life was like. These stories come directly from my heart—or, as I might say with a wink and a nod to the name I grew up with, from the *hart*.

Anne Hart Preus

Gravel and Grits

Sometimes we joked that we lived so far in the country, we had to have sunlight pumped in. The distance into the country from town, on the gravel road seven miles to my home at Hitt Spur, made the journey one that not everyone cared to take, so a person had to be going there with a particular purpose. Hitt Spur is located about halfway between Webb (then population five hundred) and Parchman, the state penitentiary. The gravel road sometimes had too much gravel, making the navigation difficult, and it sometimes had no gravel. At other times the water got over the road so deep that a car could not pass. Neighbors were a few miles down the road—way beyond a "stone's throw." The gravel road was always a challenge. It kept the flow of traffic to a minimum, and so we were both isolated and insulated in our own little world in the country. It also provided a cloud of dust whenever a car or tractor passed by, so we made friends with the dust and didn't worry about things being dust free. We had many skinned knees and elbows from the rocks when we learned to ride our bikes, but we always picked ourselves up and dusted ourselves off and got right back on the very thing that had demoted us to the ground. We were stubborn, with heads just as hard as the rocks on the gravel road.

Traveling on the gravel road was not done frequently, so groceries were bought in town on Saturday or grown in the garden. Daisy, the cow, gave five gallons of milk a day, and churning it would give us buttermilk and fresh butter. (Milk was poured into the churn, and a wooden stick with a wooden cross attached was used to pump up and down until the butter rose to the top. The butter was then scooped up and molded with a butter paddle and squeezed until all the milk was out and then, voila, butter. I did not know that milk could come in a carton all pasteurized and homogenized, and I would not drink it after Daisy the cow disappeared. It took a long time to get used to the store-bought kind. Even butter did not taste the same when it came from the store. Actually, we bought margarine, and my taste buds had been primed for that real butter. The butter paddle not only shaped the butter, but it shaped behavior as well. Mother found it to be a valuable resource in readjusting our attitudes.

Chickens provided eggs and drumsticks, and pigs contributed bacon, sausage, and other pork delights. There were no Wal-Marts or big chain grocery stores. The local merchants kept tickets, and at the end of the month those in debt paid up. There were no Visa cards or debit cards then, either. Credit was on a person's word.

Good food was the standard, and no meal was complete without meat, four or five fresh vegetables, cornbread, tea for the adults, and milk from the cow for the children. Some homemade dessert followed all of this so that we would leave the table "with a little taste of sweet." All food was prepared from "scratch" with no assistance from prepackaged meals or the microwave, since there was none at that time.

Sitting around the kitchen table sharing food for three meals a day was expected, and whether it was with the equipment salesmen or others who just happened to be there when the dinner bell sounded, it was a normal occurrence. If a friend happened to be around when it was time for dinner (lunch) or supper, another place setting was added to the table, and food was always in ample supply. The table would almost groan with the fresh vegetables and homemade cornbread (no sugar allowed there, 'cause Yankees cooked that way). No matter what was going on in our lives, supper would wait until everyone could come to the table. Daddy, who ruled over the table, usually delivered the blessing, which may or may not have included a roll call of relatives and friends in need of God's governance and guidance, either imagined or real. Good manners were expected: "Use your napkin and don't eat with your knife. Pass the biscuits, please." "Thank you" and "you're welcome" were required; "Yes, ma'am" and "yes, sir" were expected. There was no "yeah" and "naw" when addressing adults or anyone we might think was an adult. There was no such thing as eating and jumping up from the table. We had to wait until everyone was finished and ask to be excused from the table. We also had to remember to say we enjoyed it too.

Grits, however, were the glue that held us together. We had them in the mornings with sausage and biscuits and homemade jelly. We had them in the winter evenings just for good measure, and we never tired of them. Mother would say they would fortify us against the "elements" and because she said it, that was the law. We weren't too clear about what "elements" were, either, but we certainly wanted to be fortified in case we encountered any. I don't remember us spending a lot of time being sick—except for Will, my baby brother, and that is another chapter—so apparently grits kept us free from disease. We surely were fortified.

While food fortified our bodies, parents felt the need for spiritual fortification for themselves and for us children. Church was where we went on Sunday morning and evening. We did not go on Wednesday evenings because we were so far in the country, and schoolwork took precedence.

The world was not accessible via high-speed Internet, cell phones, CNN, or other technological advances. Those things would later become part of daily existence, but we grew up in the '50s and '60s, before the advent of such conveniences. We received news of world or national events on the radio and through the *Commercial Appeal* that was delivered on the route by the mailman. Television did not enter the household until I was six years old, and reception was fuzzy at best. Cable, satellite, CNN, and FOX were all things of the future and not a part of our lives.

The winding gravel road ensured that we would become self-reliant. The grits and good country cooking provided a healthy diet, and mealtimes were established routines where we learned good manners and held conversations. They were the foundation for us then and forged memories and habits we carry with us now. Isolation, good food, and regular attendance at any and all church functions marked my formative years.

Pigs and Parades

Some things could not be debated. These events were set in stone and could not be changed, and weather, illness, or acts of nature could not alter them. The Greenwood Christmas parade and the district 4-H Livestock Show, also in Greenwood, were two such happenings. A person could count on the Christmas parade being held on the first Friday of December, no matter the temperature. One could also mark down the annual district 4-H Livestock Show for the second week in March to coincide with schools' spring break so children would not have to miss school to mingle with the cows, pigs, and sheep. That may also have been a plot by those in the know to have a scheduled event to keep children who were out of school occupied.

My parents thought 4-H was a wonderful thing for us children, and Robert and Will both were given livestock to take care of. My brother Robert was involved with 4-H and had cows and pigs to show at the local and district events in the spring. Being responsible for an animal and competing for awards in showmanship, first place, etc., at the local, district, and state events instilled life skills not learned in any classroom. Because I was a girl, and my parents were very specific about gender appropriate activities, I was not given the opportunity to be around the animals. I was to be involved in the citizenship activities and with nothing concerning animals. However, as luck would have it, I was about to be thrust into the pigpen at the ripe old age of ten or so.

At the 4-H fairs, events were held in each category of animal—sheep, pigs, cows. The kids who raised them would show their animal, and buyers would then bid on them for the slaughterhouse. (We were told the animals were going to a bigger farm.)

The district fair rolled around, as it always did, the second week in March, and the Sturdivant boys were there in their usual entrepreneurial manner, selling sticks as prods for the kids to use when their animals were in the show arena. Mind you, these were just sticks they had picked up lying on the ground, though they did spend hours slightly sharpening one end so as to set them apart from just regular sticks. Nobody wanted to be seen in the show barns without those sticks—they were status symbols—so kids paid a dollar apiece for them, a lot of money then. Those boys had an eye for business then, and they still do.

Anyway, Robert got sick with the flu or something and his friend Billy Gip was sick too. It was time to show the boar hog Robert had so carefully pampered for a year, but there was no one to show this nine-hundred-pound beast. Right, you read correctly—nine hundred pounds … maybe it was more. So, here was the big hog, ready for the competition and nobody to show him because all the boys were sick. It was a fine beast, too, having been fed and pampered for a year. Younger brother Will was too little, so he was automatically disqualified from service. I don't know if I fell off the top of the pen and volunteered or whether Mother and Daddy decided that I should step into the pen and show that hog. There was a consensus, it seemed, that the hog had been too big of an investment to languish in the pen unseen.

Regardless, I soon found myself herding this huge animal into a pen with other huge nine-hundred-plus-pound hogs, and my only defense was a Sturdivant stick, which was comparable to a toothpick in that situation. I had puffed up all four feet and five inches of my young frame and marched confidently into that pen, herding that hog as though I had been doing it all my life. My knees shook, I thought I would be sick, I was afraid I would step into the pig droppings and have them forever glued to my shoes, and I was feeling extremely sorry for myself for having been forced to get into that pen with those beasts, which did not smell very good, plus I was quite scared, if the truth were to be told, when my thoughts were interrupted.

My hog, apparently, was not pleased to share the spotlight with the others and proceeded to attack the other hogs as we were parading around in front of the judges. Such squealing was quite disconcerting, and being in the middle of a group of giant, disgruntled animals was very frightening. I just froze for a moment, not knowing whether to run for the gate or stay and defend my hog. In that moment of indecision I looked up to see men running into the show arena with boards and planks to separate the hogs because they were pig rioting. I'll bet you could have heard the squealing in downtown Greenwood.

When the beasts were separated after a small eternity, my hog was done with the showtime and decided to go take a seat. Somehow, he got out of the arena and started climbing into the stands. Folks were flying everywhere trying to get out of his way. Imagine the nine-hundred-pound animal climbing into the stands, and you will understand mild (or maybe wild) hysteria.

Mrs. Ygondine Sturdivant, wife of gubernatorial candidate

Mike Sturdivant, well dressed, with her perfectly coiffed hair and a smile on her face, happened to be sitting in those stands that day because her sons, mentioned earlier, were participating in the events. To the horror of all in attendance, Robert's hog made a beeline for her. I think that for a few moments time stood still while brave men formulated a plan to rescue Mrs. Sturdivant from the charging beast. The next few moments remain a blur in my memory, and I do not remember how the men got the hog out of the stands or what happened to the other hogs or what happened to Mrs. Sturdivant. Calm did eventually descend upon the stands, though. I also remember the judges announcing the winners, and my huge boar hog was the grand champion. Mother still has the purple ribbon that says "Grand Champion" to prove it.

Somehow, I managed to accept the ribbon and prod that horrible hog out of the pen and into history. That ended my career in the livestock arena, but it was the beginning of the crazy adventures I've had in my life. I figured if I could get into that pen with all those huge, smelly hogs and survive with my four-foot-tall self, I could tackle anything. I did, and I have. Life was pretty simple … just a pigpen away from excitement. It did not take much to entertain us.

The Greenwood Christmas parade was the other event that required participation, as well as numerous blankets, gloves, and hats. The weather would always be freezing cold, but it was not a deterrent. Anybody who was anybody was at the parade, so it was a time to see and be seen. Only an extreme illness or death in the family prevented one from attending.

When I was in the twelfth grade and was part of the West Tallahatchie High School marching band, the call of the parade enticed us to Greenwood, where we saw students from all over the Delta. Bands from every school within one hundred miles came to participate. Floats were decorated by every civic organization, and even Santa Claus appeared at the end of the parade to inspire goodness in all the little children who were too frozen to go to sleep.

The parade officially signaled the Christmas season. DeLoach's and Wee Moderns were especially delighted to see the shopping begin, for they were the main stores in downtown Greenwood. Weary shoppers would stop for lunch at the Crystal Grill to fortify themselves. There, the aroma of divinely cooked food and the clatter of plates from the kitchen would welcome the diner, who would have to stop and speak to everyone on the way to a table. If you did not see someone you knew, you at least knew of them, or they knew you. Waitress Frances would oversee the dispensing of food and could juggle customers and their orders better than a circus clown on a tightrope. Mr. and Mrs. Ballas, the owners, knew every customer and their families and could not let you pay your bill without inquiring about the absent ones in the group. They were always glad to see you, and that made the dining experience at the "Crystal" even more special.

As the day faded and time for the parade approached, we would never have admitted how cold we got. After all, that is what long underwear is for, right? The majorettes did not have that option, though, and their uniforms were not designed to accommodate the long handle underwear. Neena Jennings, Jayne Henderson, LaNelle Brett, and Eva Jane Shaw were part of the majorette line that endured those coldest of days. The West Tallahatchie band, under the direction of James Donald Cooper, was by far the best one. Or perhaps we thought so, because we would have marched to hell and back for our dynamic young band director.

Young ladies who rode on the floats or in the convertibles

were stylishly outfitted in their mother's or grandmother's fur stoles. Being chosen to ride a float meant wearing a gorgeous evening gown and being the envy of all along the parade route, so no young lady would dare to shiver in the cold. Perhaps that *pageant wave* of the arm was enough to generate warmth. We blew, drummed, twirled, and marched our way down Howard Street and never knew the temperature.

Pigs and parades permeated our childhood. We knew without any doubt that the parade and the 4-H show would occur. While we could never be sure of the exact extent of our involvement, the memories are indelibly marked into our brains.

Will, front, and Robert getting Clarabelle ready for the 4-H show

Religion Ruled: God Beckoned, and We Followed (Or, If the Church Doors Were Open, We Were There)

When traveling down Highway 49 either going toward Clarksdale or Greenwood, notice the church on the side of the road by the high school. It was built by love and devotion, and it served countless families through the years with Sunday school and the assemblies where boys and girls were counted and competed against each other, Bible school, revivals, weddings and funerals. Friendships and lasting memories were forged there.

As we got older, we were expected to attend Methodist Youth Fellowship, which met on Sunday nights right before the church service. We did not live too far in the country for that, and Sunday night did not really count as a school night. If we had homework, it was supposed to be done before MYF. The only bad thing about that meeting time was that it meant we had to miss the *Wonderful World of Disney*, and I used to think how much my life would be enriched if I could just watch one program. There was also *Wild Kingdom*, presented by Mutual of Omaha. Both programs held a fascination for me, perhaps because we had to miss them for more important things. Years later, when Lanelle Brett married and moved to Omaha, we just knew she had gone to the Wild Kingdom.

Church was indeed a priority in the Morrow household. We did not need to think that just because we were on a family vacation, we would miss Sunday school or church, because wherever we were, we pulled up to the local Methodist church and presented ourselves to complete strangers for Sunday school and church. We would take home the bulletin to prove we had been there and have our attendance recorded so as to receive the perfect attendance pin at the end of the year. There is probably a drawer somewhere full of those pins.

Joining the church, too, was a "big thing." In fact, my brother Robert joined three or four times. Every time the preacher issued an altar call, Robert went down the aisle to join the church. When asked about his continued need for baptism, Robert simply replied, "I didn't want Brother MacCallily's feelings to be hurt 'cause nobody went down to the altar." Robert was only in elementary school then, but he was serious about his duty and his call. Finally, though, the preacher stopped the altar call. He must have decided Robert was the only one listening.

That was in the old church in Webb before the merger of the Methodist churches of Webb and Sumner, a small town two miles away. (The churches took turns hosting the eleven o'clock worship hour. One week the service was in Sumner, and the next week it would be in Webb.)

The Webb nursery was in the basement—yes, the basement, if you can believe that a building in the Mississippi Delta would even dare to have one. You had to go outside and descend some steps to get there, and it housed the nursery. I can still remember the smell of the basement—dank and closed up. I don't remember children ever being in there, and the mold probably would have killed them if they had. It was a strange place, and only the brave dared to descend the steps. Snakes were rumored to slither in and out, and why it was semimaintained, no one could ever explain.

The bathroom was down in the front of the sanctuary, so if you had to excuse yourself, you were on public display as you made your way to the relief station. Far be it from anyone to forget to zip their pants.

The old Webb church had a large sanctuary with Sunday school rooms along the back, and one tradition that carried over to the new church was the assembly. At the old church, Mrs. Eleanor Catoe would play the piano, and we would sing "Happy the Home." Mr. Wesley Walker was the Sunday school superintendent, and he would make announcements about coming events or church news related to the sick, injured, or dead. Ushers passed the plate and collected the offering, and Mr. Walker dismissed everyone to go to their respective classes.

I began my career at that old church as a church musician. Because Miss Nell Walker needed some relief with playing for church, I was drafted to play the new Hammond organ for the Sunday night services. Gradually I was worked into playing for the morning service. Little did I know that for thirty-eight years I would be the church organist. I was in the seventh grade at the time, and I had no clue what was in store for me in that role. It is a good thing, or I would have never been so willing to take on such a responsibility.

The two congregations decided to merge into one church, and neither facility would have been suitable for housing the merged congregations. The church fathers and advisors decided to get rid of the old Webb structure, with its exquisite antique stained-glass windows and the wonderful, massive pipe organ, which was deemed useless. The Monticello-like structure at Webb needed a lot of repair, which seemed too costly at the time. (However, it still stands and is in use today.) A building was constructed on Highway 49 beside the high school and was dedicated in 1964.

The Webb-Sumner United Methodist Church was a source of pride for the community and an inspiration to the travelers who passed by. The wall-sized stained-glass window, donated by the Catoe family, added to the statement of faith and offered hope to those on local journeys or heading to parts unknown. Charlie Whitten made sure the lights were on at night so travelers from far-off places, as well as the locals going about their routines, could see the window. It is indeed a sight to see. To find such a thing of beauty in such a rural, out of the way setting is quite awesome. The window awed anyone who might happen to be in the sanctuary around three o'clock on a winter afternoon, because the sun hit it at just the right angle to send sparkling colors from the window in images to draw one's breath. Then suddenly it would disappear and leave the viewer to wonder if indeed there had just been a magical spectacle or merely a miracle unexplainable and indescribable.

For this generation, there was little entertainment except church activities, so there was no question as to involvement in all events relevant to our age. One such event was the living manger scene on the front lawn the "New" Webb-Sumner Methodist Church in the mid-sixties. The youth of the church "volunteered" to take shifts as the characters of the Nativity scene and stand outside, in what usually was the coldest week of the year, in subfreezing temperatures. The ladies of the church made costumes, and everyone fought over the wise men's garb because it was the flashiest. Joining the cast were homemade animals that men of the church contributed. Our job was to stand perfectly still in reverent attitudes so that passersby would be inspired by the Christmas scene.

We must have been believable, since cousin Helen Hitt cried as Aunt Billie and Uncle Billy stopped to view the scene because they would not let her get out of the car to see what an angel felt like. Inevitably, a nose would itch or dare to run or the hay would tickle us, but we never shirked our duty because we knew that awaiting us was hot chocolate and homemade cookies. Those days of innocence could not be repeated now for fear of drive-by shootings or vandalism, but those memories of cold nights and camaraderie and hot chocolate will last forever. The cold, however, has been forgotten.

Rev. Tommy Poole baptizes Robert Morrow photo by Catoe

The Church in the Wildwood

Columbiana Church is in the country between Vaiden and Winona and is only opened one day a year now because all its former members have either died or moved away. No one is left to unlock the doors each Sunday or light the old gas heaters or raise the ten-foot-long old windows where wasps would dare to fly in and disrupt the sermon, as in the case of Miss Daisy Rogers and Miss Clara Caldwell, my grandmother, whom we called Bigmama (on my mother's side).

One Sunday in the heyday of the church's existence, the congregation was deeply attentive to the reverend's message when a wasp decided to intrude next to Miss Daisy. Since she was a little hard of hearing and did not know how loudly she was talking, she turned to Bigmama and said in a very loud voice, "I'm gonna get this damned wasp," and with that, she took the Cokesbury hymnal and proceeded to smash the wasp and the old window into a thousand pieces. Once everyone realized that Miss Daisy had not fallen out of the window onto the ground fourteen feet below, the laughter started and could not be stopped. Such a disturbance could only be topped by the pew crashing to the floor in the middle of the pastoral prayer when a family proceeded to crowd into one of the old pews that did not have a lot of support. The congregation tried to carry on, but the giggling eventually usurped the sermon, and church was dismissed.

No one can mistake that the first Sunday in May is *Dinner on the Ground* at Columbiana. "Dinner on the ground" was not literally on the ground (well, except for that one snafu) but outside the church on some planks built especially for the occasion. Everyone brought food—enough for a small army—and spread it out under the trees after the church service. Families competed to see just how much they could bring, and usually everyone made themselves sick trying to just sample every dish. Aunt Alma's potato salad was one of the most sought after dishes and nobody has been able to replicate it since her passing. Mother's sweet potato casserole that took a day to make and a few moments to devour was always eagerly anticipated. Aunt Kathleen's stuffed bell peppers were also a standard favorite.

However, there was one year when one of these dishes did not make it to those hallowed planks stretched between the trees in back of Columbiana Church. The church service ended finally, and the ladies began to disperse to make sure the food was ready. Aunt Kat sent her husband, Spence, to the car to fetch those valuable bell peppers. She had offered him strong—er, very strong, as only she could do—encouragement to hurry up, and in his haste to please, he lost his footing on the gravel, stumbled, and dropped the stuffed bell peppers onto the gravel road. You could have heard Aunt Kat a hundred miles away in Memphis, and Uncle Spence wished he could have been at least that far away. The sermon on tolerance and forgiveness was forgotten. A strange silence descended on the Caldwell crowd as the dishes were uncovered, and the food was served *without* the anticipated bell peppers. No "dinner on the ground" was ever complete after that without the telling of the "dropped" bell peppers.

If it rained, the planks were brought into the church and balanced over the pews, and the casseroles and fabulous desserts were gingerly placed on them. Dining was not deterred by the natural elements, and rain could never dampen the spirits of those who had come to celebrate one more "Homecoming-Dinner on the Ground" at Columbiana. Dinner on the ground was another good opportunity to visit and see relatives not seen since the previous year. Not only did "dinner on the ground" play a significant part in the development of family ties, it served as a reminder of the importance church played in the lives and habits of southern families, who cling to ritual and tradition like the kudzu wrapping itself around anything with which it comes into contact.

During the church service at Columbiana, I observed change being made in the offering plate. That was a practice new to me. I watched as Bigmama, my mother's mother, would put in a five-dollar bill and take three ones out. People could be trusted to interact with the offering there, and no one thought a thing about the practice.

The old plank church between Vaiden and Winona that was built in 1898 survived a lot of things and saw multitudes of people come and go. It still stands as a monument to the men and women of the early days of Carroll and Montgomery counties who placed God first in their lives. The singing of "The Church in the Wildwood" on page 121 of the Cokesbury hymnal every first Sunday in May evokes memories of loved ones whose voices rose in tribute years ago and which have since been silenced by the passage of years. If you listen, though, you can hear the bass of the men's voices singing, "Oh come, come, come, come, come to the church in the wildwood …" The image of Uncle Coot Caldwell singing with his hymnal, swaying from side to side, flowers from Aunt Kathleen's yard, Sara Caldwell singing a solo that shook the rafters, and the Caldwell men (Tommy and Jimmy) taking up the offering are ones that will forever be a part of Columbiana Church.

Visitin'

Some practices, traditions, customs, and habits have faded with time. The advent of busy schedules, television, and other entertainment has contributed to the demise of "visitin'." A person did not have to have an invitation to "stop by"; the coffee pot was always at ready, and dessert was always available. Sitting on the porch—no matter the temperature in the summer—and drinking coffee (no Diet Cokes then) was a time to give and receive updates on comings and goings and speculations and facts, real and imagined. There was no rush and the "visitin'" could go on for a while. It just depended on how much information there was to be shared. Children did not contribute but usually found somewhere to play, since they were to be seen and not heard. Sunday afternoons were prime visitin' times. Around three o'clock, footsteps could be heard on the porch, and Dolly and Morris Houston or Alyce and Billy Bradshaw would come in for an afternoon of conversation and refreshments. There was always a cake or pie (made from scratch) to enhance the coffee, and these were served on a china plate with china cups. A paper plate dared not appear.

Visitin' also took the form of cousins coming for the weekend, or week, depending on the time of year, what was taking place, and how old they were. Cousins Donna Townsend and Sara Caldwell would bring four or five friends from the hills of Montgomery and Carroll counties to the Delta to spend a weekend and go out with the eligible Delta boys, such as the Thomas twins. These Delta boys were very eager to escort these lovely ladies to various social events, and many a heart swooned as the "boys" exuded their charms. I thought it fascinating to see the rituals of young love and the twittering of girls infatuated with the young men. However, my presence was not wanted in the "discussion" room after dates because I was only seven or eight years old at the time.

But one night, I hatched a plan and hid under the big old bed in the north bedroom … waiting for the inevitable "spilling of guts" and the details of who said what and if that might be a prelude to future dates or not. I was in information overload with all the details of the evening and decided to make my presence known. There was a great wailing and groaning, and I was in big, deep trouble for having spied on our visitors. Sara and Donna never let me forget, and the girls never wanted to return for fear of secrets being revealed. I did extort a tiny bit of blackmail to keep some information confidential; for a small fee, I could probably be encouraged to "recall" some details.

Cousin Joe Townsend would come over to the Delta from Winona to attend Bible school at the Methodist Church, and Robert and I would then go to Winona for their Bible school and more religion. We would sings songs like, *"Deep and wide, deep and wide, there's a fountain flowing deep and wide."* "Itsy Bitsy Spider" was a favorite, too. Other songs that brought out the songbirds in us were *"Jacob's Ladder," "This is the Day"* and *"This Little Light*

21

of Mine." We might not have had the right notes, but we certainly made a joyful noise.

Bible school would last from eight in the morning until noon. In early years we would go for two weeks, and then it was condensed to one week. There would be a graduation program on Friday night for parents to attend, and we would receive beautiful certificates after singing our favorite songs. We would gather up our projects like the matchbox covered with shells or the popsicle stick crosses we had glued together. Oh, the art projects we did make, and those were probably the springboard for Joe's artistic nature to take hold because years later he would paint scenes form Winona and place permanent memories of places held dear in magnificent watercolors. Yes, visitin' was important and helped us bond as family and as friends. It isn't practiced so much anymore because the world has changed. That time before TV and fast paces was special.

Visitin' was not limited to children or teenagers, either. Adults visited for overnights or weekends too. Frequently, the Hatfields from Memphis would come for the weekend to Hitt Spur just to escape the hustle and bustle of the city. Dr. Hatfield was our pediatrician, and he and Mrs. Hatfield had two children around our ages. One night, the grownups were in the living room, along with a few added friends, and we children were in the boys' room right off the living room. We had exhausted our repertoire of entertainment when the idea of playing circus popped into our brains.

We decided to play tightrope walkers, and so we proceeded to tie a rope from the bedpost to the chest of drawers, which we thought was quite sturdy. We fastened the rope securely, and someone "volunteered" to be the first tightrope walker. The selected person proceeded to get on the bed and make the first step onto the rope. We were all admiring the courage of this individual when the loudest crash erupted. Adults came running from everywhere to discover the huge chest of drawers on the floor and us in a circle staring at what could have certainly been disaster for the selected tightrope walker.

There was a long period of silence until the adults ascertained that no one had been hurt, and then the questioning began. "What were we thinking?" "Did we know someone could have been seriously injured?" The answer, obviously, was no. We did not deliberately set out to injure anyone—just to have a little fun. Fortunately, angels were guarding us and prevented harm to us that night.

For the rest of the evening, the door to the boys' room was wide open and adults periodically checked on us before we were sent to put on pajamas and report to bed. Any thoughts of anyone in that crowd wanting to be a tightrope walker or even associate with the circus were forever put to rest. That experience put all thought of running away and joining a circus out of our minds. Yes, visitin' could be very, very exciting.

Gifts and Gaffes

Uncle Billy was Daddy's brother, who came to the Delta in 1947 to farm with him, forming Morrow Brothers at a place known as Hitt Spur in Tallahatchie County. He was the Delta's most eligible bachelor and lived with us until I was ten years old; thus, I had three parents. There was nothing Uncle Billy enjoyed more than a good story, fine food, and exquisite clothes. Living life to the fullest was what he was all about, and every day, every moment, was an adventure to be savored and shared.

He and Daddy had grand ideas about gifts, and one year they purchased a brand new International tractor for Mother's birthday. I can still remember how very *excited* she was to receive a new tractor, all red and shiny and huge. I do believe she failed to consider the thousands of dollars that piece of equipment cost, though, because after the extreme excitement such a gift brought, there was a period of *extreme* silence in the household.

The International tractor salesman, Mr. Dawdle, was afraid to appear for weeks. He could usually be counted on to arrive around lunchtime on a weekly basis, and his absence was duly noted. I think that forever afterward, he and Daddy conducted business on the front porch, out of the range of Mother's hearing and gaze. Mr. Dawdle knew the atmosphere was a little tense when Mother "forgot" to bake a pie or cake to have with the afternoon coffee and sales pitch.

Then there was the other gift, and it put a screeching halt to the extravagant gift giving practice. It was the day the bull arrived. Uncle Billy and Daddy raised Hereford cattle, and it seemed there was an urgent need for a full-blooded Hereford bull, or so they thought. In their zest to provide a wonderful gift for Mother and Daddy's anniversary, they traveled to Winona to George Harris's sale and were the top bidders for this prized bull. In their excitement over obtaining such a fine beast, however, they overlooked the fact that this might not necessarily be the perfect gift to celebrate a wedding anniversary. When the bull was delivered to the farm, all the workers and we children were awed and amazed at such a creature. To show how very special he was, he got his very own pasture by the barn. Uncle Billy told me the bull would need a place to rest, and the barn was convenient. When Mother was summoned to view her "gift," she was less than awed and amazed, and that was almost the last anniversary she and Daddy celebrated. However, that was the last of the wonderfully extravagant gifts of a farm-related nature, and their marriage lasted sixty-plus years. Minus any bull, that is.

Fresh milk straight from the cow assured us of having all the butter and milk we could drink, and Daisy was the cow that was so kind as to provide it. Robert Pittman was in charge of the milking process, and sometimes Mother would do the milking. I can remember trying to "help," but Daisy would have none of that and promptly kicked over the bucket containing the milk. I was an observer after that.

Dinner parties were a common event at our house, and

entertaining was *the* thing to do. I was not allowed to be at the big table, but for years the story was told about the great gaffe. Everyone at the dinner party was having a great time, enjoying the excellent dinner prepared by Mother and reveling in the conversation, which turned to names. One of the very dressed-up ladies mentioned that her middle name was Daisy, and Uncle Billy immediately chimed in, "Why we once had a cow named Daisy. She gave gallons of milk a day. Every good cow should be named Daisy." He realized his error, but it was too late, and the climate at the table became quite chilled. I do not think those people ever returned to Hitt Spur, and Uncle Billy never got over his embarrassment. It did not stop the dinner parties or the entertaining. It did, however, stop Uncle Billy from mentioning cow names.

The Flag Inn in Tutwiler was a great place to go for a twenty-five cent hamburger, not to mention the fact that it had the most magical red, vinyl-covered bar stools at the small counter. They could twist and twirl with the slightest of movement and with just a little more energy could rapidly accelerate into quite a turbine of energy. Those stools were just waiting … and Uncle Billy would not disappoint.

One night Uncle Billy and Aunt Billie had taken Robert and Will, my brothers; Dora Sue, Billy Gip, and Hugh Gregory Clark, our down-the-road neighbors who were our ages; Helen Hitt and Bonnie Claire, their daughters; and me to that infamous dining establishment on Highway 49. We were getting situated, ready to order, and the children were on the red, vinyl-covered stools. We had tried out the spinning cycles on the stools, and Uncle Billy had asked us to be still and stop spinning because he didn't want us to fall off or hurt someone else or get on his nerves (there's that phrase) any more than we already had.

Another family or two had come in to eat, and one of the

children obviously had not experienced the rapture the spinning stools could bring and was proceeding to work his stool into a jet engine, turbine-whirring monster when Uncle Billy glanced up from his booth across the room, saw that someone was disobeying, and promptly jumped up, jerked the child off the stool, and said in his sternest voice, "Didn't I tell you not to do that?" The child erupted into tears, and Uncle Billy immediately realized that it was a strange child—not one of the crowd he had brought—and was so embarrassed.

He began to look around the café, and the mother started toward him. He had no idea what to expect from this lady, but flight entered his mind. She said, "I am so glad you did that. I had warned him about those stools before we came. Now maybe I won't have any more problems." With that she jerked the child up and marched him to the table where she was sitting. You can believe the stools remained still after that, and this incident illustrates that it was all right to expect good behavior from everyone. Misbehavior was not tolerated, and all adults were to have respect and authority. Uncle Billy gathered us up and quietly ushered us out the door. I think we could have heard a pin drop, it was so quiet. It was a very long time before we had hamburgers at the Flag Inn in Tutwiler.

Juvenile delinquency, misbehavior of any sort, or disrespecting elders was not an issue or a problem in those days. Everyone felt responsible for monitoring any child or teenager at any time or place. Good behavior was expected or there would be a reprimand or a phone call to parents and public humiliation over the daily/weekly coffee drinking gatherings. One's good name was a prize, and a slight smear of scandal was for those on the other side of the tracks and not for respectable, fine, upstanding citizens—no matter how far in the country they lived.

A small town had some drawbacks, but in the instance of child rearing, there can be no comparison. I used to dream of the day when my life was not an open book and where nobody knew me or my name or my parents. I am not sure what I thought I would do, but the familiarity of the small community was overwhelming and suffocating at times. Now, I realize how that community "interest" shaped and formed and provided my values. No parent wanted to be the subject of the conversation at the Rotary Club or Lions Club or United Methodist Women because their child had done something unthinkable. Peer pressure was not only on the child but on the parents as well. Small towns thrived on gossip, and it did not take much to set the wheels of information or disinformation on track. If there were no funerals or weddings to anticipate, the time was ripe for tales, and no one wanted to be the subject of those news-breaking tidbits. FOX News was not needed then because breaking events made it all over the community in a matter of minutes.

Uncle Billy and his Thunderbird with E.V. Catoe, Jr., looking on

Characters Cast from Many Molds

Small towns could not exist if it were not for the colorful individuals who did not ebb with the flow but marched to the tunes of different drummers. Some were a little daunting, others comedic, but all were awesome in their own right.

No matter who won or where the game was, one fan could always be counted on—Dee Da. He never missed a West Tallahatchie High School athletic event. He rode his bike and bummed Coca Colas from anyone who would spare a dime. I am not sure of the farthest distance Dee Da rode his bike, but it seemed that we couldn't go anywhere without running into him. If we didn't run into him, then someone else would mention that they had traveled somewhere else, and the first person they saw was Dee Da. (Dee Da had been injured at birth, which caused some slight deformity in his appearance as well as in his speech). He was known as a "character," and he could always be counted on to welcome the Greyhound buses at the Blue and White service station … that is, until the day when he got on a bus, sat in the driver's seat, and with his warbled, rough speech asked, "Hey, where ya'll wanna go?" People evacuated in large numbers, and the driver, who had taken a rest break to get a stage plank and an RC, thought someone had planted a bomb because people were exploding out of windows and rushing out the door … until he investigated and found out it was Dee Da who had been sitting in his seat and caused such havoc.

Dee Da also loved to direct traffic after ballgames, especially when there was a funeral. Once, there was a very large funeral at the Webb-Sumner Methodist Church, and cars were lined up for miles. Dee Da had parked his bicycle and was out on Highway 49 stopping the oncoming traffic so the funeral procession could make its way onto the highway and toward the cemetery. Cars were backed up to Glendora on Highway 49 and almost to Tutwiler in the north. Anxious to please some of the waiting crowd, Dee Da waved some of the waiting vehicles on to join the funeral procession. One of those was the Wells Fargo truck, which joined the funeral procession and proceeded as far as the turnoff to the cemetery. For years, people joked with one of the prominent lawyers in the community that they had thought it was his funeral and he *really was* taking his earthly rewards with him via Wells Fargo.

Other stories exist around the community about Dee Da, but no one ever spoke about him in an unkind way. He would have done anything for anyone, and his good nature ingratiated him to all.

Other characters wove their impressions around us like an embroidered cloth, each leaving a stitch, or leaving us in stitches, as the case may be. Miss Eunice practiced the art of hairstyling and occasionally "did" eyebrows. When I was in the eighth grade, Mother decided I should have noticeable eyebrows (I was blonde and had eyebrows, but they did not show up) and took me to Miss Eunice for a beauty enhancement. The reddish black dye she streaked across my forehead might as well have been the scarlet letter, for the stark contrast of those bold lines created an indelible mark that I could not scrub off with Lava soap. I was so embarrassed I did not want to go to school, but I had no choice but to bravely face the laughing mob who thought I looked like some mistake. If I could endure that, I could endure anything. Mother did not attempt to have my eyebrows dyed again.

Miss Eunice was quite skilled at finding out and sharing information (gossip) and could have you spilling your guts about the most secret of secrets before you even realized it. She would lean over you as she was winding your hair around those brush rollers and, in her soft voice, say, "Now, tell me about Sally Jones," and whatever came to mind would be blurted out before you could even think. Or she would ask, "Did you hear about the bank Sally Jones robbed?" and in an effort to set the record straight, you would blurt out your version of news on Sally Jones. The CIA could have used Miss Eunice to ferret out information from the most reluctant of prisoners.

She gave many a permanent and dyed many a head of hair that delightful blue color. Shampoos and sets were only a quarter. Miss Eunice was also a problem solver, and she used those Diamond Red matchboxes to cover her customers' delicate ears while they sat under the hair dryers. Rest assured, Miss Eunice knew how to take care of her customers, and no problem was ever too great for her. She is probably giving the angels a shampoo right now.

The other thing about Miss Eunice was that she had a fishpond in her yard. It was maybe five feet by three feet and had lily pads and other water plants, along with some very big goldfish. That pond was a source of mystery and speculation, probably due to the hints dropped by Miss Eunice herself. We were never sure exactly how deep that pond was, and it was suggested that it even went to China. There was a deep respect for that little pond, and we dared not get too close to the edge because we were not quite sure how it would be in China, but the sight of those goldfish and the mystery of the pond itself fascinated us and entertained us while Mother had her hair "done" in the beauty parlor.

The "beauty parlor" no longer exists. Instead, there are "salons" with hair spray—not spray *net*—but there are not any places with fishponds to entertain small children during the beauty enhancement process of their mothers.

If you needed a good laugh, Billy Nail was the one to go to. Or he might even find you if he needed an instant audience. He always had some cartoon in his pocket to pull out, and it might have been on the "questionable" side or not, depending on his frame of mind at the time. His mission in life seemed to be to cheer people up, and he did just that. His quick wit presented a challenge to one and all. He worked at Turner Brothers on Main Street in Webb and was the world's best salesman. His famous line was, "Ya'll come on in. We've got everything marked down. We've got eight-foot stepladders marked down to five feet." Billy worked there until the doors closed, and then he was employed in the tax assessor's office to provide a watchful eye on the comings and goings of the local citizenry. He could always be counted on to provide an upbeat comment or an interesting aside on the political issues of the day. Whether they were "politically correct" or not was a different matter. But one thing was for sure; you would not leave an encounter with Billy Nail without a smile.

Another memorable fixture in the community was Pang, an immigrant from China who settled in the Mississippi Delta and, like other Chinese people, opened a store to provide for his family. His store was in Sumner on the square right across from the Confederate soldier statue. Pang's family lived in the back of the store and worked seven days a week from sunup to beyond sundown. They even delivered groceries in town and thought nothing of a request to deliver ice cream to some tired, hungry children at ten o'clock at night. Of course, the delivery did not come without cost: That pint of ice cream probably cost six dollars back then. He just put it on the tab, and you settled up at the end of the month.

Stories abounded about the extent of Pang's wealth. One such story was told about a farmer who had forgotten to get payroll from the bank on Friday for his numerous tractor drivers, field hands, mechanics, managers, etc. The farmer went to Pang and told him of his predicament, and Pang, in his usual deferential manner, said, "Ah, no need to worry. I have amount in safe." And with that, he opened the safe and took out the requested money. It was never known at what interest rate the farmer had to repay the loan, but he was able to pay his employees and was forever in Pang's debt after that.

Pang's store had well-stocked shelves, considering the store was in such a small town. He carried just about any item a person would think of needing, but if such an event happened that someone might need, say, a can of smoked oysters that was not on the shelf, Pang would immediately say, "I don't have it today but will have it tomorrow." You could bank on the item being in Pang's store the next day. It did not matter what a customer requested, Pang would have it as if by magic the very next day as promised. Some people thought he was part magician, but others knew he was a shrewd businessman who knew what customer service was all about. How he was at the store all day and then managed to retrieve the requested item was and still remains an enigma.

The Pang store is still on the square in Sumner, but it is no longer open. When Pang's health deteriorated and he moved to California to be with family, other family members tried to carry on in Pang's tradition, but it was never quite the same. There could only be one Pang.

Other people entered and exited our lives, and I was fortunate to have them as part of my existence. They inspired me to laugh, to dream, and to wonder as they taught me patience, tolerance, and an appreciation for differences. Sometimes people would shake their heads at a particular individual and say, "They lost the mold on him/her." Truly, they were one of a kind. Every small town is enriched by its "characters," and we were truly blessed to have had more than one.

Two Brothers

Family is and always has been important. Our identities, personalities, philosophies, and quirks are shaped by the ones who spend the most time with us and offer guidance and direction in whatever capacity is needed. Family is our barometer for the world and identifies us as, "Oh, you're Choc and Dink's daughter." Kinship is more binding than superglue.

Being the oldest, and the only girl, had both advantages and disadvantages. I learned at an early age that I would have to "direct" my brothers. Robert was born two years after me, and I was not happy about his intrusion into my life, so I tried to erase him by sprinkling baby powder all over him, but he was not to be so easily gotten rid of. An adjustment to my attitude with the butter paddle by Mother prompted me to be more excited about him, and thoughts of having him disappear vanished very quickly. Will was seven years younger, and I have finally forgiven my parents for not having a baby sister for me. I have come to love and appreciate both brothers and would not trade them for anything.

Expectations were hard to live up to, and I was expected to do the right thing always, to set a good example, and to wear dresses. My parents were from the "old" school and thought girls should be girls and boys should be boys. I was allowed to wear shorts in the summer and pants in the winter under a dress. I did not own a pair of jeans until after my sophomore year in college. Will did not follow the "guidelines"; instead, he became the first "streaker" in Tallahatchie County. In his early years, though, Will would not be seen without those black rubber boots with the red circle around the top. He did not mind that he had them on the wrong feet or that the temperature outside was one hundred degrees or more. We would eventually miss Will and find him asleep under the tree in the yard. When it was time for rest, Will took advantage of any spot.

Robert just rolled with the flow. He liked to play cowboys and Indians and could be coerced into playing "school" from time to time with Dora Sue and me. Robert caught the attention of the high school cheerleaders and was tapped to be the mascot for the football team. He wore a football uniform and the cheerleaders would drag him across the field in front of the team at the beginning of the games. He reveled in those cute girls' attention and did not notice that his arm was almost pulled from the socket. The scales for weighing the cotton sacks fell on Robert, and Mother used to say if his head wasn't so hard, that accident would have killed him. Thank goodness for hard heads. Robert never wanted to go to bed and was quite the night owl—just the opposite of Will. Mother would have to get the butter paddle to "convince" Robert to go to bed. We knew that morning would soon arrive, and the yellow school bus would not wait on sleepy-eyed children to board.

I am thankful for two brothers, opposites in many ways, yet alike in that they no longer need my "direction."

*Celebrating my graduation from West
Tallahatchie High School in May 1967*

Two Billies

Not many people are blessed to have an Aunt Billie and an Uncle Billy. Uncle Billy was Daddy's brother, whom he affectionately called "Buddy," and when he and Daddy moved to the Delta to begin farming, he was single and lived with us. He was quite the eligible bachelor and eluded many pursuing females until Billie Hicks caught his eye. He was forty-five at the time. He and Billie got married at Bellevue Baptist Church in Memphis in September of 1959 in a wedding I'll never forget because I got to wear my very first high heels and my feet hurt so badly I could not listen to the preacher, who was extremely long winded and spoke about everything in the entire Bible before he pronounced them man and wife. He dragged the rib out of Adam and preached all the way until the New Testament when Jesus turned the water into wine. I then had an Aunt Billie and Uncle Billy.

Uncle Billy had the first Thunderbird in the whole county, white and very sporty. He even took me to the opera *Aida* in Memphis and let me ride in that vehicle with his date. I thought I was as grown as I could be. He loved fine things and taught me to appreciate music and good food like artichokes. When he married, though, he gave up the Thunderbird because he always said he wanted to be a married man with an Impala. Dinah Shore would have been pleased. Dinah Shore was a singer, actress, and television personality in that era, and she made a commercial for Chevrolet. The key phrase was "See the USA in a Chevrolet."

Aunt Billie was from the big town of Sledge. She had taught math and met Uncle Billy when she was secretary to the Baptist Hospital administrator in Memphis. They had two daughters, Bonnie Claire and Helen Hitt. She and Uncle Billy loved people and Mississippi State and rarely missed an opportunity to entertain or attend an athletic event at State. Their energy level was on high, and they would go to a game at State, get home past midnight and be at Sunday school the next morning. They would always include Robert, Will, and me on various trips. Fun was their motto, and living life to the fullest is what they did.

Aunt Billie and Uncle Billy Morrow in September 1959

Dink and Choctaw

Annie Laurie (Dink) and James Hart (Choctaw) Morrow are responsible for me being on this earth. Two finer parents could never be found, and for sixty-plus years they have been there for me.

Mother and the butter paddle are synonymous. She could walk faster than anybody I ever knew (except her sister Kathleen), and her footsteps could echo throughout the house, so we would know without question that someone had erred but was soon to be put back on track. The butter paddle could do that, and we knew not to run because that would make the punishment worse.

Mother was a child of the Great Depression and did not believe in wasting anything. She delighted in cooking and working with flowers to create spectacular masterpieces to please the eye and the palette. She created decorations out of cotton bolls and used her talents for the benefit of weddings and the church for more than fifty years.

Daddy was quite the individual. We did not know until our late adult years that he had lost his hearing when a bomb exploded near him during World War II in France. He was passionate about his country and was determined to do what he could to honor it every chance he had. He was active in scouts, the Lions Club, from which he received the Melvin Jones Fellow award, the American Legion, and the church. He wanted us to see other places and meet other people to diversify our experiences. Daddy did not believe in getting in a hurry and kept his own schedule. We were usually late for things, but it never did bother him. We got there when we got there. He did not feel that a map was anything to bother with, so many trips were taken that led to detours and delays until we could find the way to our destination. One way just meant "his way," and stop signs were simply meant to be for someone else, while he "hesitated" at the intersection.

Mention "Choctaw" and there will be someone in the room who knows him. He never met a stranger and never forgot a name. He remembered a birthday, too, if anyone ever mentioned having one, and he sent many a college student a church bulletin to let them know they were thought of. Family connections were quite dear, and we would spend hours looking up some relative that no one had seen for years. A more sentimental human could not be found.

Roles were clearly defined in his mind and not to be waived for any reason. Girls were to be feminine and taken care of and to take care of the home and not be subjected to any horrors of life, such as branding cattle or seeing their horns removed. Girls were not supposed to wear pants, literally or figuratively, and that was the way it was.

My father was a soft-spoken man who avoided conflicts as much as possible. He never spoke an unkind word about anyone, and that is a trait to be admired. The best in actions and appearance was what he looked for in people, and it was what he expected. He still gets up and puts on a tie, even if he is not going anywhere. A tie is what a gentleman wears, and a gentleman he is to the very core.

My parents provided rich experiences for us and taught us to broaden our horizons and to look further than the Delta sunsets. We value family, connections, history, and the past because these things were important and were emphasized.

James Hart and Anne Hart Morrow photo by Catoe

Part of the Family but No Kin

Clara and Robert Pittman watched over us like guardian angels; in fact, there were many times that they proved to be heaven sent. Robert Pittman came to the house before the sun came up and started the coffee to wake everyone up. I must have had coffee before formula because Robert Pittman would stir up a special mixture for me that was mostly milk and a lot of sugar and a wee bit of caffeinated liquid. Clara would follow a little while later so she could get Will and hide him, and he would not have to go to kindergarten because Will could see no rhyme or reason for school in any form or fashion. During cotton harvest time, Will would conveniently disappear into Clara's cotton sack, and by the time he surfaced, kindergarten was well under way. There was a special bond between Clara and Will. They were both individuals with strong spirits and determination.

Robert Pittman could do anything and was not afraid of hard work. (I say his whole name because my brother was named Robert and we had to distinguish who we were talking about.) He was an essential part of our household, and he worked in the yard, around the house, babysat us (along with the collie dog), and drove a tractor. His talents even included making the best melt-in-your-mouth biscuits to go with venison he had gotten at the deer camp. He had served time in Parchman when there was no such thing as prisoners' rights. Parchman was modeled after the plantation system, and the prisoners had to work in the fields under the watchful eyes of the trustees, who meted out justice and discipline for the slightest infraction. Just surviving showed what a strong individual he was. I know now that the tunes he hummed softly as he went through his daily chores were ones from the days on the chain gang. The haunting sounds and melodies were signals of the pain and suffering he had endured, but those pains and sorrows were never displayed in any way but through devotion to our family. We were equally devoted to him in a way that many people could never understand.

Robert was there the time I unlatched the screen in the breakfast room and tumbled ten feet onto the bricks below. Mother came unglued, thinking I had surely killed myself, so it was Robert who calmly left the kitchen to go outside and scoop me up in his thin ebony arms. He saw the gash on my head and told Mother, "Miss Annie Laurie. We gotta get this child to a hospital." Since the nearest hospital was Parchman, the state penitentiary, off we went. The doctor sewed my head up and said I was lucky my neck wasn't broken from such a fall.

Robert Pittman and Will were the best of buddies, and he called Will "Buddy." He would take Will ridin' around in his old blue International truck. One day, Will came home from ridin' 'round all dressed up, like he was going to a wedding or a funeral, but he was definitely dressed up. Robert Pittman had charged the stylish ensemble to Daddy at Double Door Turners (Turner Brothers) on downtown Main Street in Webb with the help of the world's best salesman, Billy Nail. Will has probably not been so dressed up since that day, so we should have grabbed the Kodak camera and snapped some pictures. Very few pictures exist of Will in his young days, since he went "on a spell" and tore up all of his pictures that he could find one day when his black rubber boots must have been too tight. We regret that the Kodak was not put into use to capture *Will in a Suit* for posterity. That portrait would have surely made it to some auspicious art gallery.

Robert Pittman lived to be a hundred years old, and Will, Mother and Daddy, and I attended his one-hundredth birthday celebration in Clarksdale and reminisced about old times. When he passed away a few weeks later, Will represented our family at the funeral that lasted hours because so many people wanted to give remarks and be part of the occasion.

Clara worked around the house too. She was in charge of Will, and that was a full-time job. Robert Pittman helped on the farm during the day, so someone had to keep an eye on Will. She would charge comic books at the drugstore on Saturdays and bring us all sorts of treats that we loved. She could also cook the best cornbread, served with wonderfully red Kool-Aid. We thought Mama could walk fast, but Clara could run a close second. We could be outside playing and get stuck in a tree or get into some difficulty, and Clara would appear as if by magic to rescue us and give a strong lecture. Her words were law, too, and we listened. She had a sixth sense when it came to protecting us, it seemed, and we were grateful. She also served as buffer when our difficulties touched Mother's nerves. "Now, Miss Dink, them children didn't mean no harm," she would say. And by some miracle, Mother would soften.

Clara was a shrewd individual when it came to managing children, although she and Robert never had any of their own. We would play vacuum cleaner, which entailed us taking turns chasing each other around the house with the vacuum cleaner. Of course, the rule was that the hose had to be on the floor; thus, housekeeping and entertainment would be accomplished all in one fell swoop. Our fear was that someone would lift the hose up and suck us into wonderland or somewhere less fascinating.

One night, Clara was babysitting us along with the preacher's children at the parsonage. We were running and playing chase all over the house and working ourselves into quite a level of excitement. Clara had tried to engage us in a quiet activity, but we were past quiet, so we expanded our chase game to the outside. In the frenzy of playing chase and slamming doors, one of us accidentally put a hand through the pane of glass in the back door, and blood shot everywhere. Clara grabbed a kitchen towel and wrapped the injury before calling our parents. We settled down then, and Clara dared us to move while she tried to stop the bleeding. Our parents soon arrived and called Dr. Lacey, who came and sewed up the wound before giving us all a stern lecture.

Clara and Robert were part of our existence, and we took for granted that they would always be around. Clara would leave us first in a way we were unable to comprehend: the cigarettes she craved got the best of her, and lung cancer took her life. Robert, Will, and I are enriched for having Clara and Robert Pittman in our lives. They nurtured and protected us, and laughed and cried with us. They showed us dignity, tolerance, and wisdom every day.

Hugh Gregory Clark, Robert Pittman, Will Morrow

Treks, Trips, and Times to Remember

Summers were to be treasured, consumed, and enjoyed to the fullest, and every one was an adventure in and of itself. Whether we took a vacation to the Florida coast, just journeyed to the hills of Carroll and Montgomery counties to visit relatives, or ventured farther than ever from the Mississippi Delta, our experiences could never be rivaled by the most creative of Hollywood movie producers.

Going to the beach was a summer ritual that several families enjoyed. The Bradshaws, Penningtons, and Hatfields usually managed to gather at the same place with us. We would load up in the station wagon and, yes, Dora Sue and Billy Gip (our down the road neighbors), would come too, drive to Destin, Florida, to the Capri by the Sea Motel and stay a week. I never understood why Mother thought it was not a vacation to have to cook three meals a day in that tiny kitchenette, predominately using an electric skillet, deal with wet towels and sunburned bodies, and sand in the bed for a week. We probably won't need to mention the gallons of Coppertone sunscreen we had to bathe ourselves in, either. I myself had a blast ... that is until our imaginary crop dusters created havoc with the hamburgers. To be sure, though, we learned some valuable lessons.

Billy Bradshaw was grilling hamburgers for the combined families, who were enjoying a social hour overlooking the beach, and Billy Gip and I were playing crop duster. There may have been a few other "crop dusters" flying around, but ours were the only two of distinction. You play this game by grabbing fistfuls of sand and extending your arms and "flying" around over the countryside, slowly releasing the sand as you "poison" and dust the crops. We were flying all sorts of maneuvers and having a grand time, gathering larger amounts of sand with each maneuver. A slight breeze had started as the sun was setting. We just happened to get a little carried away with our game and got a little too close to the open grill where the hamburgers were sizzling, and we "poisoned" the wrong thing. Billy Gip and I soon realized our error and tried to make amends, but there was no such thing. There is not one way in the world to retrieve sand from half cooked hamburger meat, and the more we tried, the more sand we got into those hamburgers.

There were a lot of mad people that night, and I don't remember if we ate the sandy hamburgers or just did without. There were no fast-food restaurants to run to for replacements—just a small grocery store. That was before the days of high-rise condominiums and wall-to-wall businesses and traffic that is bumper to bumper. My vocabulary was increased as Billy Bradshaw discussed how he felt about the crop dusting of the hamburgers, and the other adults joined in. Needless to say, Billy Gip and I had our pilots' licenses revoked in a hurry, and the crop dusters remained grounded for the rest of the vacation.

We were right down on the beach, and the adults could sit outside in the early morning, drink coffee, and watch the waves while we slumbered in our sandy beds. The drone of the air conditioner hummed as the adults relaxed and enjoyed visiting while the tide rolled in and out. Since then, developers have demolished the Capri by the Sea to make way for fancy high-rise condominiums, and there is more than one grocery store and restaurant to provide sustenance to the hungry beachcombers. Convenience is readily available, but it is not as appreciated as the meals prepared in the electric skillet in the tiny kitchenette or the hamburgers not "poisoned" by eager crop duster wannabes.

Summers passed by with lightning speed, what with the trip to the beach and a week in Winona with Grandma Morrow and another one with Bigmama and Papaw in the country between Vaiden and Winona and then a few days sprinkled with Aunt Alma and Uncle Coot. Each visit was extraordinarily entertaining in its own unique way.

Town was Winona with Grandma, Aunt Lallie, and Aunt Fannie, two old maid aunts of Daddy's, in the big brick house on the corner of Summit Street and Highway 51. That was before the days of the interstate highways, and all the traffic going north and south in the state came through there. Sounds of big trucks' brakes as they made preparation to stop for the red light kept a small country girl awake. Robert and Will did not spend time in Carroll or Montgomery counties in the summer; I am thinking the reason was that they were unmanageable for older people, and since I was the angel, I got to enjoy other places. There surely could be no other answer.

Grandma would take me into town, and Aunt Fannie and Aunt Lallie would accompany us too, the four of us making quite a quartet as we traipsed around town. They all wore shirtwaist dresses with those black lace-up shoes with the square heel. Aunt Lallie with her dark glasses and silver hair, along with Aunt

Fannie, who was like a dainty bird, helped Grandma entertain me and made sure I did not wander into the street or pick the poppies in the yard. Grandma would also take me to the library, where I would explore all sorts of worlds through the books. The library smelled old and dusty, and the books seemed to be waiting just for me; I was especially interested in Egypt and the mummies and could not read enough about those subjects. The library was a source of entertainment, and I looked forward to those visits.

We would all load up in the green '53 Oldsmobile and cruise around town for our entertainment. That car was huge and had no power steering so it is a wonder Grandma could even drive it, but she did, and we had a lot of fun watching as people hurried to get out of our way. I would sit in the back seat with Aunt Lallie, and it seemed like we were a football field away from those in the front. Aunt Fannie rode shotgun and Grandma drove because she was the only one with a license. I think we rode around a lot because there was no air conditioning, and we could get in that big car with the windows down and at least have a breeze on our faces. On Sunday afternoons, when there was not much traffic on Highway 51, we would get in the Oldsmobile and go to see the buffalo—yes, buffalo. I do not know where the buffalo came from, or why they were there, but they provided an outing on a quiet Sunday afternoon.

We spent endless hours in the yard watering flowers and collecting things for the scrapbook because we had to make one every time I went. We used all sorts of things for the scrapbook, like church bulletins, greeting cards, and pressed flowers and leaves between wax paper to create lovely works of art. There wasn't any TV so we had to pass the time some way. They did not believe in using too much electricity, so when it got dark, it was time for bed. Sometimes in the twilight, Grandma would play the baby grand piano for Aunt Lallie, Aunt Fannie, and me in the sunroom. There, in the waning shadows of the evening, the sounds of the piano muffled the noise of the traffic, and we were entertained in classical fashion.

Sometimes the Townsend cousins would take me to the city pool for a swim. Their mother, Aunt Kathleen, was Mother's sister, and she was quite a character in her own right. She would always have something to talk about and usually at high volume. She loved the Methodist church and her flowers. Her African violets and roses were the envy of everyone. I do believe she could walk faster than any other human being. She would walk to the Piggly Wiggly and to church because Aunt Kathleen never learned to drive. Uncle Spence was a fixture on the front porch as he rocked in his favorite rocker and dispensed opinions to anyone who happened by. Uncle Spence was a devout Baptist, which caused some consternation among the Methodist Caldwells, but they allowed Aunt Kat that one mistake. The smell of Old Spice cologne and Brillcream will forever be synonymous with Uncle Spence. He and Aunt Kat were quite a pair.

One day, Uncle Spence came roaring into the driveway on two wheels from church and stormed into the house and in his loudest voice asked Aunt Kat, "Who the hell is Lottie Moon?" You would think such a good Baptist would know that information, but he was highly disturbed at the amount of attention Lottie Moon got in his church and wanted and demanded some answers. Aunt Kat was able to answer, being the good wife and Methodist that she was.

I don't know how it was determined when I would go to the country, but when I did, my city days ended and an even quieter life took over. Bigmama and Papaw's house had floors where you could see through to the ground. Taking a bath consisted of putting hot water in a tin tub and splashing around and not being concerned about modesty and privacy, but the tin tub disappeared when they built a new house. I spent my "country" time between Bigmama's and Aunt Alma's since they were only two miles apart. Both were divine cooks, and no food ever tasted so good as theirs after a hard day of playing in the gullies and fishing with Bigmama and going to the barn to shell corn for the pigs.

Bigmama was not afraid of snakes, and she would tell me, "They are more afraid of you," but I didn't bet on it and did not look for an opportunity to test her theory. We saw a lot of those critters, but they never fazed her one bit. We would sit on plastic buckets and cast our bait out into the pond, waiting for some poor fish to pounce on it. Usually Bigmama would catch the most, and we would have fish for supper. My *catch*, however, consisted of those that had just graduated from minnow school. I did not want to take part in the preparation of the fish for consumption and would try to find somewhere else to play.

We always had a great time tromping through someone's pasture to a favorite fishing hole, and every fishing trip had its special story, but the time Bigmama took me to Aunt Peg's pond was perhaps the most exciting. We had gone over to Aunt Peg's house and been stuffed with all kinds of special desserts and were ready to fetch our poles, bait, and buckets out of the car, but the car had disappeared. We thought someone had stolen it, and since Uncle Earl worked at the courthouse and had an inside track on law enforcement, he called the sheriff's department to report it. While we waited for "the law" to arrive, I was gathering up rocks to throw into the pond when I noticed something in the water. I looked again, called for Bigmama, and we started down the hill toward the pond to investigate. Lo and behold, there was

Bigmama's car … almost in the middle of the pond. She had left it in gear at the top of the hill, so instead of catching fish that day, we had to fish the car out of the pond. I was sworn to secrecy, but Aunt Peg's lips were not sealed, so the tale was told countless times, to Bigmama's chagrin.

Other sources of entertainment included "listening" on the phone, for eight families shared a phone line called a "party line." There was no need for wiretapping, since we could tell who was receiving a call because of the ring. Then, we would just pick up the receiver and listen to the conversation, and all kinds of news could be scooped by being very quiet. The brave listener could also enter into the conversation—thus early versions of conference calling began. Bigmama's source of entertainment was the party line, and she spent hours listening in and catching up on all the gossip.

Aunt Alma had three children: Jimmy, Sara, and Tommy, who were all older than I. Sara allowed me to play dress-up in her old prom dresses, but there was a particular one that I loved and wore every time I visited. It was a long lime green with some sort of lace trim, and I thought I was Cinderella when I put that dress on. There were some others, but that was my favorite. Jimmy was occupied with work and school, but Tommy would allow me to follow him around sometimes, and since I had no big brother, he served as one. Even though they were a few years older, they still took time to pay attention to me, and I was in heaven.

Saturday nights had a ritual not to be interrupted for any reason. Nothing, and I do absolutely mean nothing, could interfere with *Lawrence Welk* or *Gunsmoke,* and everybody from both households—Bigmama's and Aunt Alma's—gathered around the black and white TV to see those programs. The only sound interrupting them was the buzz of a mosquito or the ting of Uncle Coot's tobacco spit hitting the side of the cup or fireplace.

Days with the relatives, however, could not rival THE trip West, for it was there that amazing discoveries were made. Fast food was not something readily available in the country, and I was sixteen years old before I had a taco or piece of pizza. We had never even heard of a taco until the family took the trek to California in the station wagon for the International Lions Club meeting. Now, that was the adventure of all times. Three weeks of driving and stopping to see every "hysterical" (actually, historical, but as we saw millions of these, they became hysterical) marker between Webb, Mississippi, and Los Angeles, California, was a vacation to top all vacations. Chevy Chase himself could not have invented such a trip.

It was the summer of 1966, and racial tensions in the nation were at an all-time high. Little did the Morrow family know that as we were driving around Los Angeles in our Mississippi tagged vehicle, the riots of the Watts neighborhood were waiting to erupt. Daddy had gotten a little misdirected and, of course, would not stop to ask directions, so we drove around for a while … actually, it was more than awhile. It seemed like days. We were aware that people were stopping to stare at us, not only because the station wagon was totally out of place, but because our pale faces and Mississippi tag were like neon signs. Where were the GPSs? We just drove around until, by some miracle, the right road appeared, and we were in another part of the city. Some guardian angels must have guided us out of that territory, and now I know what Custer felt like when he encountered the Apaches. We were definitely not in friendly territory.

In Sacramento, Daddy wanted to show us the state capitol (because we had seen every state capitol from here to eternity on the way out there). It did not matter that the building was on a one-way street, and we were headed the wrong way; we were to see the capitol, no matter what. We were begging him to turn around, and he just said, "I'm driving one way, *my* way." And he kept driving until we said we had seen the capitol. Horns were blowing and people were shaking fists, but it never fazed him. His mission was accomplished. He said, "People will see our tag and know we are lost. They'll excuse us 'cause we're from Mississippi." We had added one more capitol to our list.

Other events, like meeting Lee Majors, star of *The Six Million Dollar Man* television show, touring Hearst Castle and Yosemite National Park, and seeing the Pacific Ocean, made indelible marks on us. We were truly in a "different world." The mountains and ocean were quite different from the flat Delta, where a person could see for miles. We had our first taco at Hearst Castle and the first bite of pizza, and we were initiated into a world yet to be explored—the world of fast food. Those things were unheard of at Hitt Spur, and Janie's Café in downtown Webb did not deviate from the twenty-five cent hamburger and had not incorporated an international menu for its customers.

After three weeks of being on the road and stopping for every capitol and tracking down every U.S. Mint and looking up long-lost relatives, our patience and tolerance were exhausted. We were so ready to get home and have some vegetables—forget the fast food. We had begun to hallucinate about peas and cornbread by then, but we still had miles to go before seeing the Tallahatchie County sign.

We stopped at a little café in Arkansas, and as children are wont to do, we were not still or quiet, and we had to argue. The waitress came to take our order, but we were too busy fussing and fighting with one another to pay attention to her. Before we knew it, Daddy had picked up the spoon and had thrown it at us, and silence prevailed for the rest of the trip. He was not one to raise his voice, but the spoon incident was forever etched into our memories, and we knew that eventually Daddy would reach the end of his rope, but it would not be an end we would like to experience. The rest of the trip was pretty quiet because we were not sure if a hidden spoon might appear and orbit around the station wagon.

Finally, the magical sign, *Tallahatchie County*, appeared, and we were home free. We had crossed the desert, explored the Wild West, tasted different cuisine, met movie stars, viewed historical landmarks and experienced different places, but the flat Delta fields and endless horizon were a scene we were not willing to trade at any cost. The smell of the earth and the taste of black-eyed peas were worth more than any taco or slice of pizza. Home began to have a special meaning and a special "feel" for us, and we knew that no matter how far away we would go, home for Robert, Will, and me would forever be on a gravel road between Parchman and Webb. That trek west was a chapter unparalleled in the family book of vacations.

Bound Only by Imaginations

Imaginations knew no bounds, as a spot beneath a shade tree on a hot, sweltering summer afternoon provided a kitchen to bake mud pies and cakes. That spot was also good for using sticks to "plow" fields and grow imaginary crops. Dora Sue Clark (my neighbor from a mile or so down the road) and I would spend endless hours in her back yard under the huge old tree that provided shade and prevented the grass from growing. We would sweep that area and imagine a kitchen, where we could "cook" up all sorts of concoctions with water and mud and perhaps a few rocks for decorations. Sometimes we collected leaves to add a little flair to the mud pie. We would place them gingerly in the "oven," which might be under a chair or in a box or just on a makeshift shelf, to bake until "done." Then, we would invite our brothers to "taste" those delicious concoctions.

Oh, the play parties we did have! There was an unending supply of dirt, water, and hot sun to provide the necessary ingredients for such events. Play was never ending until the last rays of sun settled behind glorious orange and purple sunsets while the fireflies and mosquitoes emerged to take over the night. We played in the yard without fear of child molesters or kidnappings. We also took turns spending the night in an unceasing desire to make the most of summer vacations.

A cardboard box became a magnificent doll house with interiors especially designed with ads from the latest Sears catalogue. What castles could be built using a few boxes stacked in assorted designs and converted to a house with photos glued inside. When that scenery grew too boring, it would be discarded and another house constructed. Imagination had no limits. Perhaps because we did not have TV, we were forced to invent our own entertainment, creating worlds that only we could know, unspoiled and unscathed by outside influences.

I also had dolls and played with them sometimes. Tiny Tears was my favorite, and then along came Barbie, and Tiny Tears was put away. I really was not that interested in any of those dolls, though, and preferred to read in my pink room or just play outside. The pink room was my refuge, and I spent hours sitting on the floor with a book, transported to other places. The world could have come to a complete stop, and I would have never known it when I was absorbed in a good book.

Brother Will was quite easily entertained as well. In the waning days of summer, he enjoyed going to Aunt Billie's and Uncle Billy's, where he would spend hours putting rocks in a circle in the carport to house the woolly worms that were everywhere. He would choose a few to tame and keep them captive in the rock circle. Will and the woolly worms would entertain everyone.

Cowboys and Indians could go on forever and might lead to a game of football or baseball. Sometimes, chasing the crop dusters as they dropped DDT on the crops would provide a diversion. It was never too hot for us to be in the yard or running up and down the turn rows. The sweat would trickle down our necks and create circles of dirt around our throats, but we didn't care. We would run into the house for a few minutes to get a drink of cold water, and it was right back out the door so fast that we were out of hearing range when the screen door banged shut. Most of the time we went barefoot, which gave us a sense of freedom beyond comparison.

Games like hopscotch, red rover, and drop the handkerchief entertained us in the yard or at school during that fabulous recess. Sometimes the thick Delta dust was marked with hopscotch squares. It did not require many materials except a piece of concrete and some chalk, or a rock could be used to scratch off the squares in the dirt to jump into. You threw a marker and hopped on one foot to that square, picked up the marker and hopped back if you could manage all of those motor skills.

Red rover required that you divide into teams where the team members stood side by side with arms linked to form a chain. Teams faced off against one another across a span of yard. The captain would yell, "Red rover, red rover, send Robert right over," and Robert would run as fast as he could across the yard or field straight into the opposing team and try to break through the linked arms. If he was successful, then he would choose a person to take back to his team. If he could not break the chain of arms, though, he would be required to join that team. The winner was the team with the most members.

Drop the handkerchief was another of those challenging games, requiring a handkerchief or napkin or even a scrap of cloth. Players stood in a circle, and the person chosen to be "it" stood on the outside of the group with the handkerchief. "It" would skip around the circle and finally drop the handkerchief behind someone, who then had to chase after the person who dropped it. The goal was for one person to squeeze into the empty spot and the person left out of the circle was "it." Then the game repeated.

Outside was where we lived in the summers from sunup until sundown when the days lingered on, and the hot, humid days slid into sultry, sticky nights. That was before the days of cell phones, so we had to be summoned inside by Mama calling us from the porch. We could be waaaaay down the road, but we knew that voice and knew that it was time to make a beeline home. It did not do for us to invoke any sort of ire, so we scooted and scrambled home as fast as our legs would carry us. After hand washing, there was a good hot supper on the table, and we gathered there, blessed the food, ate, bathed, and climbed into those crisp, clean sheets that had been dried outside and smelled so fresh. There is nothing like sun-dried linens—a little rough, perhaps, but divine. Our tired bodies, soothed by a comforting bath, took solace in those luxurious sheets and offered no resistance to the sandman, who stood ready to whisk us away into dreamland. Another day had slipped into our memories.

Anne Hart Morrow, Dora Sue Clark, Robert Morrow, Billy Gip Clark

Will Morrow, Hugh Gregory Clark

Winter Wonderland—Better than Disneyland

Winters descended on Hitt Spur and brought entertainment that only we could invent and that Walt Disney could only marvel at. Cold weather did not deter us from outdoor activities, and as long as I. Peal's store and Turner Brothers' on Main Street in downtown Webb kept an abundant supply of black rubber boots with the red rims around the tops, we were out the door. Every year or two we would have a significant snowfall, which set our minds in motion of how to best enjoy the fluffy material that afforded us some time off from school.

Marinee Pennington, who was a friend of my parents, was the instigator of several activities and made sure that we enjoyed each and every moment. Mother or Daddy would take us to town to Marinee's house, and we joined her children, Jim and Hedy, along with Betty Bradshaw and Jane Shaw and a few other town kids. Marinee would tie the hood of an old car to her jeep, and we would hop into the hood so she could pull us all over town. It was the Webb version of a sled, and the slick snow would double the speed at which we traveled up and down the streets, over the railroad tracks, and through Main Street.

There had to have been guardian angels watching over us, for it is a wonder that we did not smash into a tree, since Marinee did not have the words "drive slowly" in her vocabulary, and she pushed the jeep's accelerator to top speed. The rope tied to the hood did not have any controls, so we were at the mercy of the fates. Screaming at the top of our lungs only made her go faster, and we loved it. When we finally did stop, Marinee would fix hot chocolate to soothe our throats and warm our bones. We would rest for a few minutes before tackling something else because we certainly did not want a second of the day to be wasted.

Another "sledding" activity consisted of getting a cardboard box from the Western Auto and cutting it into squares so we would all have a "sled" to go down the railroad tracks or the bayou bank. The only thing about the bayou bank—even though it had a sharper incline—was the water that we might accidentally slide into if we could not stop our powerful boxes. We would slide down the banks until the box became soggy and then make another trip for more sleds to the Western Auto, where owners Katherine and Hub Maxwell did not mind our recycling efforts and cheerfully contributed to our fun with stove and refrigerator boxes. Marinee encouraged us to find higher hills, and we tried to meet the challenge. The Delta did not have much to offer in the way of a hill, but we made use of every bump or incline.

These inspirations for Disney rides could not match the excitement we felt when the opportunity presented itself to be world class Olympic figure skaters. During one particularly cold winter, the temperatures hovered in the teens for several days in a row, making ice out of all water on the landscape. Long Slough, which was across the road from our house, was a shallow body of water that froze solid. Of course, the temptation to walk on the slough was more than we could stand, and eventually Dora Sue,

Billy Gip, Hugh Gregory, Robert, Will, and I were out there sliding around in our rubber boots and pretending to be skaters.

Aunt Billie, who was ever ready to entertain us, found some ice skates that she had worn when she lived in Memphis and brought them to us. They were size eights, but we did not care. We just stuffed socks in them until our feet would fit, and for Will and Hugh Gregory, that was a lot of socks because they were the youngest. We had two or three pairs of skates, so we took turns. Standing on those small blades was quite a challenge, and when we fell down, we could not get up. Thank goodness we were not very tall, so the distance to the cold surface did not bother us too much. After a lot of practice, we mastered standing up for a brief period and then easing around the ice. We spent most of the time on our bottoms, but we had on so many layers of clothes to cushion our fall that we didn't care. We just knew the world was waiting for us to skate onto its stage.

Being active and inventing entertainment consumed most of our snow time, but eating always had a way of being part of the schedule. Mother would scoop up some untouched snow, add a little vanilla flavoring and some sugar, and serve snow cream. There was and never has been anything quite like that snow cream. It certainly hit the spot after a long day sledding or skating.

The snow and ice lasted much too briefly, and the school doors opened, putting a halt to our Olympic preparations. We would have time, though, to plan and imagine some other ways to enjoy the snow when it fell again. We cleaned the ice skates and stored them in the closet, knowing that the next time we pulled them out, we would not need so many socks.

Irrigation: to Water the Fields and to Cleanse Our Souls

A necessary part of the farming operation entailed irrigating the fields if Mother Nature did not cooperate by providing adequate rainfall during the growing season for the cotton and beans. The irrigation pipes would be hauled from the shop and carefully placed along a predesigned path, and the irrigation well would churn into action and produce countless gallons of ice-cold artesian water laced with just a little iron. The crops seemed to do an about-face when that water began to flow through the fields, and new life was infused into the cotton, which needed just a drink to survive during the sweltering heat of the Delta summers.

The irrigation ditches served as excellent swimming holes, and we never hesitated to jump right in … that is, if we had on clothes that did not mind the iron rust of the water. We had to keep an eye out for the water moccasins, but with all our splashing about, the snakes took cover somewhere else. We had no idea that people actually swam in real swimming pools with chlorinated water. That was not a reality for us. The hot summers would be unbearable, but the cold artesian waters of the irrigation ditches revived us and cooled us off for a brief period.

There were other forms of revival as well; we learned about the spiritual one and took part in that with any opportunity. Maybe because we didn't have too much else to do, or maybe because parents thought it was preventative medicine, we went to all revivals at Friendship, which was the Webb Baptist, Sumner Baptist, and Methodist churches.

My parents had insisted that we go to the revival at the Webb Baptist church because some of their members had filled up a pew or two at ours a few months before, so off we went in the station wagon in our Sunday best. The Friday night service marked the end of the revival and meant that several converts would be baptized right then and there, so as not to allow any time to change their minds. Will had escaped the revival and stayed with Clara Pittman, but Robert and I were on the front pew so we wouldn't miss anything, and we took note of the entire ritual. Our eyes were as big as saucers when Brother Riser held the convert under the water for what seemed like a very long time before bringing him to the surface. The young man emerged from the baptistery gasping for air, and maybe for freedom, with hair and robe soaking wet and a wild look upon his face. We were not sure if he had seen Jesus or just been scared out of his wits that he might drown. Brother Riser had said, "Mr. Smith has come to know and accept Jesus" before they had gone to the baptistery.

We sang "Amazing Grace" for a long time (like for a hundred verses), and the preacher and the new member made their way to the front of the congregation after taking off the baptismal robes. Mother had made her way to the pew with us as a precautionary move, since Robert was prone to join the church when any altar call was issued. To be sure, it was a new and different experience for the Methodists, who chose to be sprinkled with a few drops of water as a route to salvation. Complete immersion was a thing to be pondered by tiny children with big imaginations.

Perhaps it was the beating down of the summer sun upon our little heads, or maybe we were just out of things to do when the idea of playing church entered our brains. We had been playing hopscotch in the turn row that ran alongside the main irrigation ditch, and we were pretty hot and sweaty. It just seemed the "thing to do," as if we were all drawn into the same thought by the swirling, ice cold water meandering its way through the cotton field. Dora Sue asked, "Anybody wanta play baptizin'?" Since we were not sure exactly how baptized we would be, we were reluctant to answer, but she put the pressure on us and the idea into our heads. One by one, we agreed.

Of course, church would not be complete without the baptizing of a fresh convert, and since Will was the youngest, he was chosen. Dora Sue and I were the choir, Robert was the usher, and Billy Gip was the preacher. Hugh Gregory was the congregation. Since no baptism was complete without *the* book, Robert was sent back to the house to get the Bible so we would be official. We found a couple of sticks that we made into a cross by getting some Johnson grass and using it as twine, and we stuck the cross into the ditch bank. The stage was set.

Billy Gip was a little reluctant in his role, but after prayer— "God is great, God is good. Let us thank him for our food"—he began to assume his importance. We sang "Deep and Wide" and "Row, Row, Row Your Boat," because those were the only songs we remembered from Bible school. Billy Gip opened the Bible, and we tried to say the Twenty-third Psalm, which we had learned in Mrs. Grantham's room. We got almost through the whole thing before he called for anyone who wished to be baptized to step forward, and since Will forgot, we gave him a gentle nudge.

Billy Gip took Will's arm and walked to the edge of the ditch, where they perched atop the clods of gumbo dirt, and he reached down and got a handful of the ice cold liquid to baptize Will. The shock of the water caused Will to stumble slightly in his black rubber boots. The clods of dirt forming the ditch bank were hard as stone, and he lost his balance. In his attempt to grab hold of something, he caught Billy Gip's arm, so they both went reeling over into the ditch.

We just stood there taking in the scene. The ditch was a little deeper than we'd thought, and all of a sudden, Will was under the water—held there by the sucking motion of the water filling his rubber boots. Billy Gip was in shock and kept bobbing under the water, gasping desperately. It took a few seconds for us to realize that this wasn't playing and that Will's baptism might come in pretty handy in a timely yet unplanned manner.

Dora Sue took charge and made us form a chain like in red rover so we could reach over and get Billy Gip, who could then get hold of Will and pull him out of the water. The clods of dirt were like concrete and made navigating the ditch bank almost impossible; that gumbo dirt had baked in the sweltering sun and was not going to crumble. It seemed like years passed before we got them out of the ditch, and by then the commotion we had created caught the attention of the farm workers, who came running for all they were worth to see what we were doing.

Clara Pittman lived at the end of that turn row, and she turned into a supercharged racehorse when she heard the commotion, knowing that a disaster might be happening. She was like a lightning bolt running down that road, and when she made it to where we were "baptizing," she let go and cussed a blue streak.

She grabbed Will by the arm, with the rubber boots making sucking noises from all the water, turned him upside down so the water would drain from the boots, and dragged him all the way to the house. Mother took over and the rest of us sat on the porch in fear and dread that the butter paddle would appear and send us all straight to hell.

Irrigation of the fields continued, though, and the crops grew to produce a record harvest. The congregations at the small churches also increased as new converts were baptized with reviving waters, and our thoughts were forever cleansed of any notions of playing "baptizing" again.

Intruders in the Roses

Growing things were important to the ladies in my life: Mother, Aunt Kathleen, Grandma, Bigmama, and Aunt Alma. For all, a garden was an important and necessary element, key to the existence of the family. They all worked gardens until they were forced by advanced years to stop, and they all loved flowers—especially Aunt Kathleen and Mother, who provided flowers for almost every social event in the community. Weddings, showers, parties, or church services were not complete without the beautiful flowers grown by Aunt Kathleen or Mother. A competition of sorts evolved between the two of them in the rose division. Each one prided herself on her roses and on whomever had called to request them to decorate for an event. The event was a source of competition as well, because a high-society wedding topped a small bridal shower.

For two women who had grown up in Carroll County during the Great Depression, a simple flower evoked a sense of pride and accomplishment and offered a genteel acceptance into a more secure world. Mother volunteered to fix the flowers for church for fifty-plus years and spent every Saturday and early Sunday mornings rounding up flowers or plants to put on the altar. Her arrangements were works of art and labors of love, and she spent many hours getting the arrangements "just right."

Mother had made a large rose garden in the yard since her flowers were in such demand, and she received so much enjoyment from sharing with others. At first, there were only a few rows of roses, and then slowly more rows of fragrant flowers were added, and the rose garden encroached into more of the yard. No one cared, though, because Mama was happy. When Mama was happy, everybody was happy, and the world spun along. She spent hours poisoning and pruning and tending to those roses. That is, until the day someone forgot to fasten the barn gate.

The barn was just across the road from the house, and the pigs stayed there to receive their food and water and to wallow in the mud hole they had made. They must have been impatient to see what was outside the barn, or maybe whoever was to feed them did not check to see if the gate was securely fastened, but escape from their confines they did. A simple escape was not enough. Those pigs wandered across the road, into the yard, and around to the place where the rose garden stood in all its fragrant glory. It must have been a temptation they could not refuse, for it was not long before the pigs had totally demolished any semblance of a garden, much less a rose garden. Rose bushes were uprooted and scattered everywhere, and the soil was burrowed into like a legion of gophers had been through it. It was a disaster that no tornado could have created. It looked like those pigs had a mission to find and destroy because they zeroed in on that portion of earth and proceeded to dismantle it.

Mother had been to town and came home to tend to the roses and discovered the damage. Words cannot truly and adequately describe what she said or did. But suffice it to say she was madder than a hornet, I can tell you. Everyone on the whole farm took cover and made themselves veeeeery scarce. There was a lot of tiptoeing around and whispers and glances, but no one ever confessed to letting the pigs out of the barn, and it was a wise person that decided to remain quiet, you can be sure. That mystery remains.

It was a sad day in Hitt Spur, for the rose garden was never the same, and Mother could never reconnect with the flowers that had brought so much joy to both her and countless others. She would continue to fix flowers for church and other events, but she always borrowed roses from Marinee Pennington or Miss Polly Taylor. She could make a few roses last for a month in the refrigerator and recycled them without blinking. No one could even tell they weren't freshly cut. I don't recall whether the pigs survived or not, but it does seem that we had a lot of bacon and pork chops that winter.

Cold Enough to Kill Hogs

The farm was pretty self-sufficient, and food was grown in the garden or on the hoof. Vegetables were gathered and put in the freezer or canned, and animals were raised to be slaughtered for their meat. During the winter, Robert Pittman would monitor the weather conditions, and when the temperature had been freezing or below for several days, he would announce, "Cold enough to kill hogs." It would have to be cold enough for him to see his breath.

Killin' hogs was a major production that required all the workers on the farm to make preparations for the slaughter and processing of the pigs raised for just such an event. Hog killin' took all day, and since it was the winter, no work needed to be done in the fields, so the workers made a celebration of it. They would gather firewood and light it under the old iron pot, assemble the boards to make the tables for cutting and salting the meat, and slaughter the hogs with rifles or butcher knives.

While Uncle Billy was part of the farming operation, he had been slightly sheltered from the proceedings of killin' hogs. When his father, Grandpa Morrow, once advised him to sprinkle the meat slightly overnight, Uncle Billy took the garden hose and sprinkled the meat. Grandpa had meant to sprinkle it with salt, not water.

So even though Uncle Billy had no idea what chitterlings were, he nonetheless got it in his head that he wanted them because he had heard what a delicacy they were and how much people enjoyed eating them. As the workers were preparing for the hog killin', he instructed them to make sure all the chitterlings were prepared from the pigs. Then he went to town to the bank and post office and returned later that morning. When he asked about the chitterlings, one of the workers led him over to the big pan containing those delicacies. He took one look, inhaled the aroma, and fell flat to the ground in a dead faint. Workers came from everywhere to see what had happened, and Robert Pittman helped to revive him and get him into the house and away from the delicacies. That was the absolute end of any mention of chitterlings in our house.

Just one more mention of chitterlings, though. Once, Robert, Will, and I were instructed to get off the bus one day at Dora Sue and Billy Gip's because Mother and Daddy were going Christmas shopping in Memphis. Dora Sue had mentioned that they were having chitterlings for supper, but I was an innocent and unsuspecting child about that food. We got off the bus in our normal happy state of mind and ran into the house, awaiting our favorite snack of a cold biscuit, butter, and sugar, when the most awful smell assaulted our sensitive noses. I could not imagine what that smell was and started making all sorts of faces when Dora Sue said, "Anne Hart, stay for supper. We're having chitterlings." I could not get outside fast enough and prayed real hard for Mama and Daddy to get home quickly and pick us up before suppertime rolled around.

Daddy would always anticipate hog killin' because he would get the pig's feet, and Vorena , Dora Sue's mother, would be coerced into frying them. I don't think I was ever brave enough to try one of those either. Mother would not allow them in her kitchen, but Vorena did her good deed in preparing them. There are some things better left alone, in my opinion.

After the hog killin', the workers would prepare the meat and hang it in the smokehouse to cure. They got a share of the meat for their families, and hog killin' was over for the time being. The makeshift tables were stored, and the yard was restored to its usual appearance. No one can truly describe the sights and smells associated with those times, but rest assured that although it was almost fifty years ago, my memories of them are still crystal clear. If I never see chitterlings or pig's feet or never smell them again, it will not cause me any dismay.

The Green Bomb and Celebrations

Nothing was ever done on a small scale in my family. We did anything and everything in grand style, or at least some sort of style, and usually people noticed. From transportation to celebrations, we managed to be a little different. Some things were part of our existence because of necessity and others were because we just loved an adventure and a chance to spread our wings a little. Uncle Billy and Daddy were always waiting behind the scenes, or on the scenes, or in the scenes, to offer encouragement and advice.

The Green Bomb was a huge 1953 Oldsmobile with no power windows or steering that provided us with transportation to school and was easily recognizable as the Hitt Spur car pool machine. When Grandma Morrow could no longer drive, Daddy brought the Oldsmobile to the Delta because it was too good to get rid of, and so it sat waiting for me to take the wheel. We gave it the nickname "Green Bomb" because it was large, green, and dangerous. There was no need for an airbag in that car because it was built like a tank.

The legal age to get a driver's license was fifteen, but that birthday passed, and I was not a licensed driver. I did not want to drive and was petrified to be behind the wheel of an automobile, but when my sixteenth birthday came and went, Mother would entertain no more of that foolishness and insisted on giving me driving lessons in the Green Bomb. That would be my first and last lesson. We were rolling along on the gravel road approaching a ninety-degree curve, and Mother said, "Now, you need to slow down." I thought slowing down meant going from fifty to forty-five, which I soon found out was still a little too fast to navigate the hairpin turn with no power steering or power brakes.

The Green Bomb went airborne and sailed over the ditch, landing right on top of some very fine cotton plants. Mother was not amused, but since we were not hurt, I was thinking that it was a good thing we had not been hurled into outer space. The Green Bomb was not damaged, either, and we were just a little shaken up. Robert Pittman was in the field plowing, came to our rescue with the tractor, and pulled the car back onto the road. Mother got behind the wheel and chauffeured me home in silence; she was finished with driver's ed. Uncle Billy and Daddy were waiting to see how the lesson had gone, and when they heard the story, they just sighed and said, "Well, that's all right."

We abandoned the yellow school bus as a means to get to school every day and instead rode in style in the Green Bomb. Dora Sue, Billy Gip, Robert, and I caught everyone's attention as we eased into the student parking lot. Not only did we have a ride—which was unusual because not many students had cars then—but ours was a classic and was big enough for a whole class. When I graduated from high school, Robert took over the Green Bomb and even took it to Southern when he went to college. Just as bicycles liberated us from the confines of the yard, the Green Bomb launched us into different avenues. Our horizons were broadened further, and the world became just a little closer to Hitt Spur.

No mile was too far, no hill too high, no task too great when the Morrows wanted to do something. Take Christmas, for example. Nothing, from getting the Christmas tree to visiting Santa and even our Christmas wishes, was within the usual. Not only did Mother decorate in a large way, she had to have the perfect tree, which meant that we would load up in the pickup truck and go to Bigmama and Papaw's to storm the woods in Carroll County for *the* Christmas tree. Papaw would put us in the lift on the tractor and off we would go through the hills and valleys, yelling at the top of our lungs because Papaw would not slow down for a ditch or gulley but go full speed, almost slinging us into another state. Then we would traipse through the woods on wobbly legs until Mother determined that we had found *the* right one. It seemed that the whole forest waited until that decision was made; perhaps the wild things of the woods did not want to be captured and taken back to Tallahatchie County. Anyway, we would cut it down and tie it to the tractor to haul back to the truck. On the way back, Robert and I would select a tree for the boys' room.

Mother insisted that her tree be flocked every year, but one year she was sick with a migraine, so Daddy and Uncle Billy decided they would take care of that for her. They got the flocking materials and put the tree on the porch and proceeded to get the tree ready for Christmas. However, they did not take into account that the wind was blowing forty miles an hour, and flocking went everywhere. The front porch, Daddy, and Uncle Billy looked like a blizzard in the Northeast had passed through. Of course, we went and told Mother, and she made a miraculous recovery. Daddy and Uncle Billy were the abominable snowmen, for sure.

When Mother finished with the flocked tree, it was beautiful.

Her gold and silver theme transformed the disaster into a work of art. Our tree, in the boys' room, was a different story. By the time we had put all our treasures from Bible school on it, made construction paper chains, and strung popcorn for decorations, the tree looked like it had been assaulted by the remnants of a lost cause. The colored lights made it all better, though, and we dreaded the day when Christmas was over, and we had to take the tree down. Robert, Will, and I would sit in that room for hours just admiring our handiwork and enjoying the magic of the season.

The decorations were just one part of the Christmas ritual. I don't think Santa appeared anywhere within a hundred-mile radius, so it was necessary to travel to Memphis to see him and inform him of our hearts' desires. One year we were getting ready, and we were at the breakfast table being encouraged to eat everything on our plates because the children in China were starving, but I was not to be convinced and would not finish my breakfast. Daddy even brought out the old airplane trick to try to get me to swallow all my food. That meant he would put the food on the spoon, turn his head, and pretend the food was on an airplane that was to land in our mouths.

Even the airplane did not work, however, and food remained on my plate, so we traveled on to see Santa and waited in line for a very long time. Finally, my turn came, and right in the middle of giving Santa my list, he stopped me and said very sternly, "Now, Anne Hart, you haven't been very good, have you?" My heart stopped, and he continued, "You must eat all your scrambled eggs if you want me to bring you toys on Christmas Eve. Just think of all those starving children in China."

For the life of me, I could not figure out how Santa had spied on me that very morning and had traveled the hundred miles back to Memphis to hear all the wishes of girls and boys in the entire Mid-South. It would be many years before Mother revealed that Santa had an earpiece, and parents could relay classified information through a microphone that was hidden from view.

Boy, was I chagrined. Mortification set in as I made my way back to the parents in absolute dismay. Will and Robert took their turns, but Santa did not have anything to hold over them. On our way home, Will announced that he had asked Santa to bring him a pig. Daddy almost ran off the road, and Uncle Billy gripped his armrest until his knuckles were white and exclaimed, "Oh, horrors!"

You can believe that for every morning after that, my plate was spotless, and I did not hesitate to consume any and all scrambled eggs. On Christmas morning, there were some skeptics who doubted Santa would deliver a pig, but Will was a believer and, when he had gotten his boots on, made his way to the backyard with us close behind. There, in front of our very eyes, was a black and white pig with a huge red ribbon around her neck. Will promptly named her Clarabell, for Clara Pittman, and the skeptics were silenced.

While the skeptics were busy finding their voices, the years passed rather quickly and high school graduation loomed upon the horizon. Parties were the custom to help the young graduate transition from the hallowed halls of high school to college or careers or marriage. Uncle Billy and Aunt Billie decided that just a regular western themed party in the backyard would not be sufficient, so they made arrangements for a senior party at the Summit Club atop one of the tallest buildings in Memphis.

Being a hundred miles away made no difference. Aunt Billie's niece, Angelita Delgadellio, from New Albany, and I could invite eight couples. We dressed in our semiformal attire and dined in quite an elegant place with many forks and spoons at our seats.

They even had an orchestra, and we danced until our feet wouldn't move and headed to our hotel (with plenty of chaperones, I might add). On the way, Billy Gip had a slight traffic incident, which almost caused him to be beaten up by a city slicker. The next morning, we had to go to court to testify about the incident. We managed to get back to Tallahatchie County with many memories of a special, yet eventful senior party. The *Sumner Sentinel* reported on the event—even getting the information correct. That was definitely the party of all parties.

The parties were a prelude to graduation, and we enjoyed a lot of them, but reality ruled, and the next steps had to be planned. Uncle Billy and Daddy decided that I would not need to take the Green Bomb to Millsaps, so they took me to the Ford place on the square in Sumner and picked out a blue Ford Torino with a V-8 engine. I think they believed if I ever got to Jackson I would not return, so they were providing a way for me to have no excuse.

That car was awesome, but I did not really like to drive, so I made my friend Jane Shaw drive us to Clarksdale or Greenwood, and when I got to Millsaps, I turned the wheel over to Mary Glasgow and Anne Babb. The traffic and multitudinous traffic lights were just too much for me. That Torino got us all to many places and stayed with me throughout my college days, but eventually it was traded in without putting too many miles on it.

It did not take a lot to entertain us, and the slightest excuse for doing something slightly different gave us *carte blanche to* try new things. Never mind that the local paper might report accurately (or not)—or that driving a hundred miles for a party was not unusual—life was different and was a joy to experience each and every day. Coupled with endearing family who served as cheerleaders and motivators, life was a blessing and a celebration!

Will Morrow: "Santa, I want a pig."

Lights, Camera, Action

There were not then, nor are there now, any traffic signals in the whole county of Tallahatchie. There has never been enough traffic to warrant their implementation.

However, being in such a rural setting did not deter us from being fascinated by the bright lights of Hollywood. There were two movie theaters or picture shows on the west side of the county. There was the Tutrovansum, named for the surrounding communities of Tutwiler, Rome, Vance, and Sumner. It had a balcony and showed such popular movies as *Hush, Hush, Sweet Charlotte*. A person could buy popcorn and candy there but had to walk across the street to the drugstore to buy a fountain Coke. We could go on Friday or Saturday night for a quarter. There was absolutely no talking while the movie was showing because there was a lady named Minerva who helped to run the theater, and she would tromp down the aisle and fuss at you publicly. She would also tell our parents at church if we had misbehaved. If we had a dose of bravery, we could sneak out the back door with our boyfriends and get a kiss, but we had to have somebody let us back in because the door locked when we went out, and we did not dare try to get back in the front. Minerva stood guard for just such wayward activities.

The old picture show in Webb, the Cassidy Theater, operated by Mr. and Mrs. Cole, entertained all the youngsters with westerns and horror movies. The theater itself was a bit of a horror because it had a wooden partition down the center that was about six feet high to keep the whites and blacks separated. That wall was just a temptation to see who could throw popcorn, candy, paper, or anything else available across to antagonize each other. Occasionally tempers would flare and disagreements would erupt, but Mr. Cole would stop the projector and quickly remove any offender, or Mrs. Cole would offer a stern reprimand, and the movie went on. The Webb picture show offered a service unheard of anywhere else; when the movie was over and the lights were turned on, Mr. and Mrs. Cole would load up the town children and take them home. Those who lived in the country had to get home the best way they could.

One afternoon I was in town spending time with my friend Joann Balkin, who just happened to live around the corner from the picture show. Mother had cautioned me *not* to see any horror movies, but that just meant that when Joann suggested we go and see *The Blob*, admonitions were thrown to the wind. I don't think I have ever been as scared, and for years I would not go to bed without looking under the bed, in the closet, and in the corners of my room because I just knew the Blob was lurking out there. When *The Mummy* played at the Cassidy Theater, I graciously declined Joann's invitation to go to the movie.

Those newsreels brought the world of fashion, politics, and entertainment in short clips to us, and we were instantly informed about world events. They were always shown before the previews and gave us glimpses of the world beyond the partition. Movies with Tarzan, Shirley Temple, and John Wayne entertained us and opened our eyes to magical and mysterious places. For a little while on those Saturday afternoons, we were transported beyond the cotton fields of Tallahatchie County.

At other times, when things were really slow, or when Mother and Daddy had company, we children would make up plays and perform them for the entertainment of the adults. We spent countless hours conjuring up characters and situations and usually allowed Robert to be the bad guy. Of course, the girls always wanted to be the most glamorous. We even put on costumes sometimes and, of course, charged admission from the adults. I believe now that they paid us just to keep us out of their way, but who would have known that?

Hollywood producers could not have conjured up such action as the Parchman escapes, though. Parchman, Mississippi's State Penitentiary, was not far, only seven miles away, and it housed the state's prisoners on a vast acreage designed to keep its tenants close. If a prisoner tried to escape, there was so much land to travel before even leaving "the farm" that the inmate would become disoriented and lost and quickly captured. However, on several occasions, a prisoner would manage to "break out," and as word spread about the "escape," local people would go and put their keys in the car, for it was felt that if they did not have to be disturbed by an escaping prisoner, their lives would be happier … or longer, perhaps.

Part of the excitement of the prisoner's escape for Hitt Spur residents was the running of the bloodhounds followed by guards on horseback galloping through the woods along the home place. They would have to stop at our artesian well to let the animals get water and of course, for themselves taste the cool, refreshing water that spewed forth from beneath the earth.

The bloodhounds were well trained and well taken care of for just such occasions as an escape. The barking of the hounds and the sound of the horses galloping down the road and through the woods were eerie preludes to the capture that would soon take place, for it was a rare occurrence that a prisoner would last longer than a few hours on the "outside." The snakes and mosquitoes were not critters a convict wanted to deal with. Sirens would scream and officers from every direction would descend to "escort" the prisoner back to serve an additional sentence for attempted escape. Even though my parents tried to shield us from life's unpleasantness and the criminal element, the capture of an inmate was too exciting to miss, and somehow we would manage to position ourselves at the well to be close to the bloodhounds and the horses, to see the big guns, and to observe the hands of justice at work.

We never felt danger, though we probably should have, but those things happened with such predictability that we just took them in stride, never thinking the rest of the world did not have access to prison escapes and captures, bloodhounds, horses, and lawmen in pursuit of hardened criminals. All we needed was for John Wayne to ride up during one of those prison escapes.

Life was never dull or boring in our rural setting. The big city could not have been more exciting, nor could the silver screen have provided more entertainment. There were a lot of things missing in our small communities, like traffic or opportunities for entertainment, but those things did not faze us as we took each moment, savored it, and committed it to our memories.

Memphis and Music

A hundred miles was nothing to travel for entertainment, enlightenment, and exposure to worlds we never dreamed existed. The magic of Memphis drew us like moths to a flame, and we could not wait until the next excuse to go there.

Some trips were regularly scheduled, and others were on impulse, but the word "Memphis" implied something magical and wonderful and "citified." When September rolled around, we knew the Mid-South Fair in Memphis beckoned, and *everybody* was there. The midway was filled with all sorts of food, but the best was the cotton candy, gooey, sticky, and decadently sweet. The circus, zoo, and the Holiday on Ice were also good excuses to leave school just a little early on a Friday afternoon so we could travel the hundred miles to the city. Downtown Memphis was the place to be in those days. There were Goldsmith's and Levy's department stores and escalators and the Peabody Hotel and other places to capture a young child's interest.

Going to the Peabody Hotel was the ultimate experience, and if we were so lucky as to be there at five for the ritual marching of the ducks, the day was even better. I could not understand how those ducks could march in and out of the lobby and get on the elevator without making a mess, so I thought I would grab one and see if it was real. That was not a good idea. There was a very loud gasp from the spectators lining the red carpet where the ducks were. Feathers flew, and hotel staff appeared out of thin air to make sure the ducks made their way to the appointed spot in the fountain and to make sure I was in an appointed spot away from the ducks. To say that Mother jerked a knot in me would be putting it mildly, but somehow calm descended on the hotel lobby after the concierge spoke to my parents and me and gently guided us to the exit.

The ducks at the Peabody still draw a crowd and are an institution carried over from a distant era of elegance and prosperity enhanced and enriched by the farming culture of the region. Planters and their families and friends sought cultural ambience in the lobby of the Peabody and in the fine dining establishments downtown. The roof of the Peabody drew people from all across the Delta to dance the night away at the Skyway. The scene for those wanting to be seen was definitely the Peabody.

Elvis Presley was one such excuse to go to Memphis, and Mother took Dora Sue and me to see him in a concert at the auditorium in downtown Memphis. We had no idea we were part of a cultural revolution and were just wrapped up in the screaming fans and the hoopla that surrounded the hip-swiveling sideburned hero from Tupelo, Mississippi. We could barely see him on stage because our seats were so far away, but Dora Sue and I never forgot that trip.

The phenomenon that was Elvis Presley created quite a stir in the households across the nation, but nowhere was he more a subject of discussion than in the living rooms of Tallahatchie

County. When he appeared on television, we drove over to George and Olivette Gates' home to watch the show. I am not sure if we had no TV at the time or if we could not get the channel Ed Sullivan's show was on. Or maybe it was just an excuse to get together, because my parents certainly liked to socialize, and any excuse would be enough.

Anyway, we gathered around the black and white television and waited with baited breath to see Elvis live on television. And there he was, but only the top half; he was blacked out from his waist down. The censors had deemed his swiveling hips inappropriate for prime-time television, but that did not deter zealous fans. Everybody had Elvis fever.

The world thought Elvis was a social and cultural phenomenon not to be outdone, but few anticipated the impact the arrival of a young British group would soon have. A few years later, when I was in high school, the Beatles erupted on the music scene, and Dave Jennings and I traveled to Memphis to see them perform. I don't think anyone heard the music for all the screaming taking place. Hysteria was truly part of the Beatles' performance; girls pulled their hair and clothes and screamed at the top of their lungs while crying crocodile tears. I had never seen anything like it.

To have been a witness to both musical phenomena was quite a privilege. Little did I know that Elvis and the Beatles would forever impact rock and roll music and initiate a cultural revolution that would know no equal. Elvis with his blue suede shoes and the Beatles with their long hair inspired a generation to supersede boundaries in all aspects of society. That time formed a citizenry unafraid of norms, always seeking answers and solutions, and leading the way to uncharted territories.

Our trips to Memphis usually included staying in a hotel

downtown. That was an eye-opening experience for Robert, Will, and me, with all the traffic, people, lights, and sheets that had not been dried outside in the sun. The fact that people stayed up after dark was something we had never known. The *country* had certainly arrived in the city. We never knew what might await us there, but we could always count on it being an adventure.

Robert, Will, Jeff and Lori Hatfield, Betty Bradshaw, Anne Hart Morrow, **back row**

Saturday Nights Live

In the spring and summer, going to town had to wait until Saturday afternoons after farm workers had been paid off for their week's labors. Cars were not plentiful, so people had to share rides on any conveyance they could find. Sometimes it was a wagon, and other times it was a truck. Main Street would be bustling and crowded with families who needed groceries or clothes or just a fountain Coke at the drugstore. It was a time when groceries, clothes, and gas could be charged on a running tab, for there were no Visas or credit cards in use then, and debit cards were certainly not heard of. The local merchants were only too happy to run up a tab and present it for payment at the end of the month. Never mind about paying. They knew the person would pay or be ashamed to show his face.

For a while on those Saturday afternoons, the tractors were stilled, and the hum of the diesel engines was silenced. No one knew anything about Wal-Mart or Kroger. Business was done locally. Stores on both sides of the street participated in offering incentives to get people to town, and it worked. Merchants stayed open until midnight, and the rival clothing stores, Turner Brothers and I-Peal's, both had customers until closing. In fact, one of the merchants would put a five-dollar bill in a jacket pocket, and when the customer tried on the jacket, he would put his hand in the pocket, feel the bill, not knowing what denomination it was, and purchase the jacket.

Both sides of Webb's Main Street were filled with busy stores in those days. Wing's Grocery, Western Auto, Bank of Webb (where you lined up to let the tellers call out your balance rather than have a printed and mailed statement), Turner Brothers (better known as Double Door Turner's), and Bill's Grocery were on the north side of the street. On the south side were the drugstore, I-Peal's Department Store, Berry's Grocery, Turner's Grocery, and Sharkey Campbell's Appliances (the oldest Philco dealer in Mississippi). Sharkey put a TV in the big window, and it drew a crowd.

The Western Auto was busy selling bicycles, washing machines, guns, toys, and other items necessary to daily existence. Hub and Katherine Maxwell enlisted their children to assist with the sales and collections of payments on accounts. Saturday, for them, was not a time to go places or visit friends because duty called, and duty was the store.

The Webb Drug Store was a popular place because it provided a spot to cool off with a fountain Coke and an opportunity to rest a bit while looking at the newest comic books and magazines. One of the county's leading citizens, who was quite a character in her own right, would drive up to the parking spot right outside the front door and blow the horn for someone to come out and wait on her. She did not seem to realize that the drugstore did not offer drive-in service, which changed slightly when she accidentally pressed the accelerator instead of the brakes and she drove straight through the front door. Glass shattered, patrons scattered, but, miraculously, no one was injured.

When dark descended, patrons parted ways on Main Street; "Back Street" livened up, and the later it got, the livelier the activity. Back Street was a back street reserved strictly for the black patrons. There was no restriction on how loud music could be, so the later it got, the louder the music got. Alcohol flowed freely, and stabbings and shootings were common, but Sunday came, and the world righted itself for church.

Both blacks and whites enjoyed shopping and visiting on Main Street. If fact, if a person had been looking down from the skies onto Main Street during those Saturday afternoons, they might have thought a giant had crushed Oreos and sprinkled them along the sidewalk.

No one seemed to mind that there was no air conditioning. In fact, air conditioning was a thing of the future then. We dressed in our starched shorts and shirts and mingled and watched each other and visited the snow cone booth until dark. The streets were filled with people eager to enjoy town after a week of hard work. Business was good, and parking was limited on Main Street. Saturdays were lively and entertaining.

Double or Nothing

The world was divided. There were two of everything—one for blacks and one for whites. The courthouse had the words "For Whites Only" emblazoned across the water fountain and restrooms. Dr Townsend, renowned for his skills in dentistry, had an office above the Webb Drug Store. When a patient ascended the stairs, Dr. Townsend, who also served as the receptionist, would bellow out, "white or black?" and, depending on the response, direct the patient to the appropriate side of the office to wait. When the Greyhound bus pulled up to the Blue Top Service Station, the colored people rode in the back.

"Separate but equal" was the rule that guided the school system, and there were schools for each race. However, during harvest season, the schools attended by the black students closed so they could work in the fields gathering the cotton, or in the gins, which ran twenty-four seven until the cotton was harvested, the stalks cut, and the fields plowed in anticipation of the next season. The lint from the gins coated the landscape, making the scene appear to be one out of a winter wonderland, and the sound of the machinery separating the lint from the seeds created a rhythm that guided the laborers and the farmers until the season ended. When it was over, the schools opened, and the interrupted dispersal of knowledge resumed. Dual expectations existed, and boundaries were not crossed, although coexistence amid calm existed, or, rather, we thought it did.

The calm was shattered when, in 1955, Tallahatchie County was thrust into the nation's spotlight with a murder trial in the death of a young black man named Emmett Till. The death and ensuing trial drew the scrutiny of the country and launched the civil rights movement. News reporters from all over the country were sent to the town of Sumner to cover the trial. People still talk about the Greyhound bus that delivered the reporter from up North, Mr. Kilgallon, to the entrance to Sumner. He had to walk the mile to the Delta Inn, where reporters stayed to cover the trial. The reporters walked across the railroad track to the courthouse to send the proceedings to the nation.

The hospitality of the local citizens never ceased to amaze these "Yankees," who came to Hitt Spur to feast on Mama Dink's most delicious cuisine. Uncle Billy entertained the crowd with stories from the farm, and the Yankees left wondering at the paradox of the Delta, which could simultaneously embrace such civility, hospitality, and horror. Other residents of the county, like the Pearsons, entertained the reporters too, for it was the hospitable thing to do. Besides, restaurants were not readily available. There was only the Webb Café and the food at the Delta Inn. To the consternation of all those who wined and dined the reporters, though, there was never a mention in their stories about the kindness extended them by the locals. For city slickers, the small town afforded no sizzling entertainment, but for the country bumpkins, the Yankees held fascination, wonder, and awe.

Betty Pearson attended the Till trial, which was a break in the norm, for women, especially white women, were not expected to take an interest in anything associated with the black community. However, Betty realized the significance of the proceedings in the old courthouse and wanted to observe firsthand what was happening. The black citizens were afraid to attend for fear of reprisals, and the whites wanted no part of the event because they thought if they did not talk about it, ask about it, or think about it, the crime would disappear. Betty's friends never asked her a word about the trial and ignored the fact that such an event was taking place right under their noses. It was the same thought, "Don't ask, don't tell," that created an unspoken code that no one wanted to break. Who knew the Till trial would forever impact the country? Those involved took the truth about the death of young Till to the grave, but the stain of violence would be visible forever.

Blacks and whites were not the only ones who were separated by culture, however. Chinese families who settled in the Delta had grocery stores, but it did not matter that the language was a barrier. Patient customers and merchants developed a way to ask for and obtain merchandise. The Chinese were not allowed to live in the community and were not invited to participate in civic organizations, so they were valued, but not vested. On the other hand, the Jewish presence was quite evident in those years. Most of the Jewish people had department stores and ran profitable businesses. They were involved in the community and belonged to the Lion's Club and other civic organizations.

Duality extended to churches as well. Hours of worship, facilities, and services were different in the black and white communities; white Sunday school usually started around ten o'clock, and the worship service followed for an hour. The minister knew that the service should only last an hour, and if he started going too much longer, the congregation would rebel, and he would be finding another congregation to serve. The black worshippers started Sunday school and church later, and the service lasted much longer into the afternoon hours. There was no time limit, it seemed, and religion continued as long as the Holy Spirit guided them.

Black baptisms added more to the service, time wise and inspiration wise. They were usually held at a river, and considerable bravery was required to go into those waters, where snakes were known to slither, but faith has a way of taking away all fears, and the singing and the support of church members could not be rivaled. The men would wade into the water and beat the surface with sticks to ward off the reptiles lurking under the surface. In our church, however, we just sprinkled a person and said a few words. The service was short and sweet and took place in the sanctuary with no sounds of sticks slapping the water. There was an option to be immersed, sprinkled, or poured upon, but everyone I ever knew opted for the least wet treatment as a way of absolving sins.

When Daddy and Uncle Billy moved to the Delta in 1947 to set up their farming operation, known as Morrow Brothers, they wanted to build a church for the black farm workers and their families. They pooled their resources and built Hitt Chapel in 1952 and provided a cemetery for loved ones' burial. Once the scene for a house full of worshippers, it now stands awaiting the faithful few who come to worship on the first Sunday of the month. The inhabitants of the cemetery far outnumber the worshipers now. For those who devoted their lives to sowing the seeds of cotton and soybeans and harvesting the snow-white bolls and soybeans, there was a place to worship and to find eternal rest in the soil they so devotedly tilled and toiled on. Hitt Chapel still stands on the side of Highway 32, between Webb and Parchman.

Mother also sponsored many weddings in those days, both in the black and white communities. One of the farm workers had a daughter who wanted to get married, and Mother offered to help with the wedding because she loved decorating and arranging flowers. The perfect setting was, of course, Hitt Chapel. Mother met with the wedding party and the pianist shortly before the ceremony and directed the pianist to play something soft and sweet for the bride's mother to come into the church. Lo and behold, she chose "In the Sweet Bye and Bye." The radio station was giving news of the community and announced the wedding was sponsored by Mrs. James Morrow. That started Mother on her service of assisting brides and their families with weddings and with decorating.

Hitt Chapel was the setting for sad occasions as well. When a member of the congregation passed, the service and burial were held right there. Time was not a factor in completing those services, and they could last for hours, no matter how hot the day was. Dora Sue and I would climb on her fence, which was only a few hundred yards away from the cemetery, to observe the activities and wonder how it could take so long to have a funeral. We were used to a few scriptures, maybe a hymn, and burial with a few prayers sprinkled along. At Hitt Chapel, emotions would run high, and, coupled with the heat, some mourners would collapse, and usually the ushers would have to fan the bereaved until consciousness returned. We were not accustomed to that sort of show of emotions in the Methodist Church. You were not supposed to cry or show sadness, or joy either.

Boundaries existed—sometimes invisible and at other times not. Unspoken rules determined one's place, and they were not made to be broken. Crossing the lines or breaking the rules was not allowed, and there were people who paid a price for doing so. Duality ruled in places of worship, schools, and all aspects of society. There were indeed differences, but the common denominator remained that the Great Creator would be there to welcome us all as we entered the Pearly Gates.

On Another Note

When Mother decided that I had to have organ lessons, she hauled me to Greenwood every Saturday morning at eight o'clock sharp to learn the finer points of playing the organ from Mrs. Sally Prosser. Mrs. Prosser professed that she was two years older than God, and I certainly believed her because she was quite frail and old. Of course, anyone with gray hair was ancient to my young eyes. Grandma Morrow gave me a Hammond organ so I could practice, and I spent many an hour getting ready for church services, weddings, and funerals. And when Mrs. Brett decided her daughter Lanelle should prepare to play the organ, she and Mother took turns taking us to Greenwood.

We would usually take a side trip to DeLoach's department store, which had a lovely Estee Lauder counter filled with all sorts of magical beauty enhancements. The saleslady, Bobbie, could make us believe we would be as beautiful as any movie star if only we bought this cream or that powder, and as an appeasement for making us get up so early on Saturdays, our mothers would end up with a huge bill for makeup. We would also go to the Frost-top and get chili cheese dogs and root beer floats. It never mattered how late we were up at Friday night football games, when it was time to get ready for the Greenwood trip, there was no excuse.

To soothe our tired souls, Miss Prosser would interrupt the lesson midway through to offer tea and cookies, and we would discuss our "love lives." She would say, "Now tell me, dear, why you have been too busy to practice?" Then, when I would relate my schedule, she would offer sympathetic advice and encourage me to put some time into my music. At other times, she would tell us stories. Once she recalled walking to her church, which was the Episcopal Church downtown and quite a few blocks from her house, when she just felt she could not go any farther. It just so happened that she was right in front of the Presbyterian Church, but she begged God not to have her collapse in front of the "wrong" church. Mrs. Prosser was a tough individual and a true steel magnolia. Her love of music and her constant encouragement opened a new door for me, and I am grateful to her for all her advice, patience, talent, and the countless cookies and cups of tea.

My organ playing provided opportunities for experiences not shared by many other teenagers. When I was in the eighth grade, one of the most prominent young ladies in the county decided to get married and asked me to play for the wedding. It was the "wedding of the year," according to many who knew what they were talking about, and certainly the most important thing I had ever been asked to do.

There were little ring bearers and flower girls and many bridesmaids and groomsmen, and the church was packed. During the ceremony, the little children decided to climb over the pews in the choir, and with their heavy-soled white shoes clomping loudly on the pews, they created a distraction to remember. Apparently they had never heard the sounds of hard soles on wood before and found it to be quite entertaining. It might have been so to them, but not to the bride, nor to the preacher, who called the bride her sister's name. One of the little ones proclaimed loudly that he did not want to be there, and the solemnity of the moment was broken. One of the groomsmen was going to try to persuade the little stompers to go with him into the choir room, but his attempt only resulted in more of an upheaval, so he left them alone to stomp in the pews. I am not sure how the minister and I got through the wedding, but the couple got married and the reception began. The couple is still married, as far as I know.

There were extremes in the weddings I played for, like the small wedding where I was told to wait for a signal from the back of the church to begin the processional. The bride had to come from home, since the church was small and had no private area for the bride to dress. I started the preludes about twenty minutes before the appointed hour and played and played and played, and still there was no signal. I played some more, and finally someone came and said they were about ready. I played a few more minutes and got the signal—forty minutes after the appointed hour. That should have been the signal that everyone should just go home and forget about the wedding, but it did happen. The marriage was shaky from the start and got even more so, and eventually a tragedy of unthinkable proportions befell the couple. It was heartbreaking for everyone and was a chapter in the lives of all that everyone wishes could be rewritten.

Other weddings were noteworthy as well—for different reasons. There was the Holy Smoke one that almost resulted in tragedy but for some quick thinking ushers. The wedding, again, was *the* event of the year, and all of Tallahatchie County and the Delta assembled in the Sumner Baptist Church to witness a favorite "daughter" unite in holy matrimony. The minister was a large individual, and there were many bridesmaids, ushers, and groomsmen, and the church was beautifully decorated with ferns, flowers, and multitudes of candles. The ceremony was proceeding without complication—that is, until an alert usher noticed that the minister's robe was smoking. He quickly grabbed a hymnal and smothered the flame and extinguished the nearby candles, and the ceremony proceeded. The holy matrimony might well have been chronicled in the *Sumner Sentinel* as Holy Smoke.

Funerals as well were challenges, and there were times when I had to totally separate myself from the event because of close associations and friendships, and had I not done so, I would not have been able to provide the music for the final tribute to a loved one. To have been able to provide some comfort playing the deceased person's favorite hymn for the family gave me a sense of accomplishment and a feeling that I was able to do "something" in such a time of sorrow. I am glad to have been able to serve in this way.

A total test of musical endurance took the form of numerous piano recitals. These required endurance from the parents to sit through the hours of plink, plink, plink on the piano and endurance on the part of the teachers, who tried to guide their young charges through the rudiments of theory and keyboard mastery. Of course, Miss Nell Walker and later Mrs. Margaurite Webb displayed the yearlong pursuit of excellence proudly at the end-of-year recital. Oh, the thought evokes memories of forgotten pieces and nervous heartbeats, not to mention the proverbial sweaty palms.

We dressed in our finest (in the early years we even had to wear evening dresses) and marched to that lonesome spot on stage, where we hoped and prayed that we could get through the piece without having to back up too many times. Eventually it would be over, and both audience and student would breathe a heavy sigh of relief. Boys and girls took piano from Miss Nell at Webb Swan Lake Elementary in that room on the side of the stage. We missed many recesses as we sought to be maestros of the instrument. The sounds of the children running and playing on the playground for recess drifted through the open window. Our sacrifices were many, but the rewards of learning a piece of music were things no one could take away.

As the years progressed, the numbers of students dwindled, but Mother and Daddy insisted that I continue the study of the piano, so the dreaded recitals continued. Mrs. Webb finally relented in the high school years, and we no longer had to memorize our pieces. Otherwise, I might be still sitting there backing up a few measures, trying to recall the piece and finish it.

The Junior Choir at the Webb Methodist Church, left. Mrs. Ruth Balkin; back, Rev. Macalilly; right, Ann Rice. Front row: Billy Gip Clark, Robert Morrow, Anne Hart Morrow, Jane Shaw, Marjorie Barrentine, Shirley Elliott; middle row: Tenny Wilson, Bobo Catoe, Dabney Maxwell, Harry Barrentine, Don Chin, Kenny Brett; and back row: Butch Little, Dora Sue Clark, Linda Little, JoAnn Balkin, Barbara Shelly, Edna Sullivan, James Arnette Shaw

School Daze

Education was valued by all the adults in my existence, and I could not wait to start school. My first encounters with the printed word took place sitting in the big green chair in the living room with Uncle Billy and "reading" the Sunday comic strips. *Nancy* was my favorite, followed by *Dennis the Menace*, but the colored strips with the strange lines inside those white bubbles all intrigued me, and I was ready for reading, writin', and 'rithmetic, or so I thought.

Unlike some children I knew, I did not go to Miss Nell Walker's kindergarten, where it was rumored that she served the coldest chocolate milk in the whole wide world and the most delicious cookies. We lived too far in the country for me to travel to town each day, so I was deprived of the kindergarten experience. The summer I turned six was perhaps the most exciting birthday ever, for just the very next month, I would launch into the world of academia and be on the road to intellectual enlightenment.

September rolled around, and parents took me to Webb-Swan Lake Elementary to enter first grade. Dressed in my plaid dress and brand new saddle oxfords, I sailed into Mrs. Lewis's class with my big fat pencil and tablet and stopped dead in my tracks, for there on the wall was my nemesis—color words. There sat Robbie Lowitz and Jerry Chin, who had been to kindergarten, and they were not the slightest bit daunted by those words. They were full of the world's coldest chocolate milk and best cookies, so were undaunted by any word—much less those horrible color words. I was ready to go back to the big green chair and the Sunday comics, but it was not to be. Mother and Daddy blew a kiss, waved goodbye, left me, and I was on my own.

Mrs. Lewis patiently introduced us to sight words, assigned reading groups, threw in a few numbers, and made sure we took our naps after lunch. But my frustration at being "behind" made me madder than a hornet, and I was determined to conquer all the information Mrs. Lewis could provide. I worked very hard and finally conquered "yellow." Spot, Dick and Jane were next, and I progressed from the buzzards to the bluebirds. There was great joy in first grade that day!

Recess was the highlight of our day, when we would run and play on the swings and make ourselves sick on the merry-go-round. Endless games of chase and red rover assured us of our daily exercise. Chase was even more fascinating when the boys decided to play … that is, until they discovered the hysteria they could cause by putting frogs down our blouses when we were caught.

Rain did not deter recess because the teachers understood that we needed to have some outlet for all our energy, so we had recess in the basement, a huge gray room with lights suspended on long poles from the ceiling creating an eerie light. The smell of Pine Sol, along with urine and wet concrete, assaulted our senses, but we were too rambunctious to care. We just did not want to be caught there alone.

There were three elementary schools on the west side of the

county, in Webb, Sumner, and Tutwiler. Each school had a peewee football team, and there was bitter rivalry. I just happened to be a cheerleader, and now that I think back … all the girls were cheerleaders. Our favorite cheers were:

- "Water in the bathtub. Pull out the plug. Down goes Sumner, glug, glug, glug."
- "Two bits, four bits, six bits, a dollar. All for the Lions, stand up and holler."
- "Watermelon, watermelon, watermelon rind. Look at the scoreboard and see who's behind."

Dances at the community house provided entertainment for us as we tried out the latest moves to the tunes the jukebox played. It would take almost the entire evening to pull us away from the wall where we stuck like glue waiting on some boy to ask us to dance. Sometimes we just got on the floor and danced without a partner.

Eventually, elementary days ended, and the hallowed halls of West Tallahatchie High School beckoned. We entered seventh grade in awe of the long hall, which seemed to stretch from Glendora to Memphis and gave the teachers and principal an immediate view of anyone not in place along the way. Mr. Logan kept order with his "board of education," and if that did not work, he would take unruly boys to the gym and have them put on boxing gloves and fight until they changed their attitudes. Mr. Logan would randomly stop boys in the hall, tell them to grab their ankles, and give them a few swats with the paddle just for preventive measures.

A new world had opened before our eyes with such things as assembly programs, pep rallies with the spirit stick, powder puff derbies, band, and all sorts of clubs. Beauty reviews and homecoming were highlights of our year. We formed friendships and went steady, and the teachers got us ready us for college whether we wanted to be prepared or not.

We should have taken lessons from the powder puff derbies. That was when the girls dressed out as football players and the boys were the cheerleaders and homecoming maids. Roles were completely reversed, and the girls were brutal. They were just waiting for the moment to tackle a rival. The guys looked smashingly glamorous in their evening gowns and fur stoles. Their genteel sides showed clearly. Otherwise, roles were clearly defined and not to be challenged.

The world was launching into rebellion regarding the stereotypical roles established for men and women, but in Tallahatchie County, the men were expected to be the breadwinners and the women were to tend the homes and be a teacher or a nurse, or perhaps a secretary. Careers were limited, and no other doors were readily open.

In the eighth grade, all girls were to take home economics and learn the finer points of sewing and cooking. According to the curriculum, sewing was introduced the first semester. We had to make a garment of some description and model it before the whole student body in the fashion show. I chose to make a jumper because I thought it looked so simple, and the pattern said "Simplicity," but the thread did not want to hold the sides together, the zipper was a little off the track, and Mother had to rescue me because she was an excellent seamstress. She was also mortified that anyone might see the disaster I had created and associate it with her. Somehow, she managed to re-create the image that was on the pattern cover, and I moved across the stage—holding my breath—and completed that portion of the course.

The second semester was the cooking portion of the course, and things moved along fairly well until the day our "kitchen" was supposed to provide the beverages for the luncheon to culminate the unit of study. Robbie Lowitz, Katy Wing, Kitty Mitchell, Linda Little, and I were one kitchen, and we were just a tad shy of being like bulls in a china closet in that arena. However, we mustered up a lot of courage because we did not want to fail and repeat the course, so we decided to make pink lemonade for the luncheon. All the "kitchens" were busy, and we had a gallon jar filled with pink lemonade enhanced with tons of sugar.

For some unknown reason, we got tickled as we were trying to move the jar to the serving area and dropped the whole thing smack on the floor. Pink syrup went everywhere, and all we could do was laugh. We were dressed up but covered in our beverage. Miss Inman did not get the joke and could not find any humor in our situation. We scurried to get the mop and wet rags, and the more we tried to clean up, the more tickled we became. Miss Inman decided to continue the luncheon without the pink beverage. The floor is still sticky, from all reports, and Miss Inman had to leave early in the semester. Rumors are that she had a nervous breakdown, but we finished the semester, and the substitute was warned not to fail us or we would be back. To this day, I cannot sew on a button, and I will burn ice cream.

Another course in endurance and fortitude was the foreign language. For those who suffered through Latin, the reward was the annual Latin banquet, where we dressed in togas and celebrated the lives of the Romans. For a week, the first-year students had to be slaves to the second-year students, and that was great fun as the second-year folks tried to think of exciting ways for their slaves to behave. We tried to make the slaves chant, "Latin, Latin is as dead as it can be. Once it killed the Romans, but now it's killing me." There was a slave rebellion, however, and the chant was never repeated—at least not in hearing range of our teacher, Mrs. Berry, which is probably a good thing.

The junior-senior prom was another event that enhanced the routine of daily school work. The juniors sold magazines out the wazoo to raise money to decorate and to entertain the seniors before they walked out the doors to futures unknown. We dressed up in semiformal attire, and the boys borrowed their fathers' cars to chauffer their dates to the school cafeteria for the banquet and dance. We danced to the tunes of the Beatles and Elvis and other hit makers of the day.

Sports were a big part of our school lives. Football and basketball dominated our interests, and those who did not play, cheered or played in the band. Rivalry between East and West Tallahatchie was fierce, and the fan following filled up the stadium or gymnasium for each game. On one crisp September night, the fans had filled the football stadium at West Tallahatchie for the annual Golden Egg competition, which incited near riots and many pranks, such as slashed tires and shaving cream on cars and busses afterwards. East Tallahatchie had come with its star player, Zack Peters. The announcer had introduced all the players for both teams, and the game started with a lot of roughness and penalties. Both teams had injuries, and players were leaving the field pretty regularly. After an especially brutal drive down the field, one of East Tallahatchie's players was not in an upright position, and after coaches worked with him, he was finally escorted off the field. The announcer, seeing that without the star player the hometown would have an advantage, enthusiastically remarked over the PA system, "The East Tallahatchie team is now playing with Peters out." The stadium erupted in laughter, and the PA system was silenced for at least a quarter. At any rate, the tension of the competition was broken for a little while.

Sports were not the only competitive events, however. Politics permeated the halls in the spring when student council elections became the focus of everyone's attention. Candidates and their campaign managers launched very active campaigns, and politics was in full force. Banners, campaign ribbons, and posters adorned both the halls and us. Students took the process seriously and listened attentively as candidates delivered oratorical masterpieces promising all sorts of things from ice cream with every lunch to shorter classes and longer activity periods. The youth group from the Webb-Sumner United Methodist Church captured the four main offices my senior year, as Billy Gip Clark (treasurer), Bobo Catoe (vice president), Jane Shaw (secretary), and I (president) were elected in a heated race. I was only the second female student council president in the school's history. Victory was bittersweet, though, for I had to defeat Dave Jennings for the office.

Politics was not limited to the halls of West Tallahatchie, as our insulated existence was soon catapulted into the rest of the nation and world when on November 22, 1963—a day none of us would ever forget—President John F. Kennedy was assassinated in Dallas, Texas, and the world changed. It was then that we realized how connected we were to events outside our small community. There were those who cheered as they heard the news because the Kennedys were considered to be so liberal, and that was an ugly word in our time. I was on my way to Memphis with Mother and Dora Sue to get my first pair of glasses when we heard the news on the radio. We really thought it was a cruel joke and that it wasn't true, but when we got to the doctor's office and everyone was trying to get the details of the assassination on the television, we realized that the news was indeed true.

A few days later, at school, we all gathered in the auditorium to watch the funeral on the old black-and-white TV, and the images of that day will be forever etched in my memory bank. There was only silence in that great big auditorium, and we were eyewitnesses to history. I still remember thinking that it was all a bad dream and that such an act could not have happened … not in our country … not to our president. Before the decade was over, the nation would experience more acts of violence with the assassination of Robert Kennedy and Martin Luther King Jr.

The days at West Tallahatchie passed too quickly, and we fifty-two were soon marching across the stage to receive our diplomas. The sounds of the night invaded the auditorium because the windows and doors were open to let in a slight breeze. Proud parents applauded as a son or daughter was recognized, and then the ceremony was over. Our lives beyond that long hall and watchful eyes of dedicated teachers had begun. The military would summon the young men to serve in Vietnam. Others would go to college or get a job. Our teachers and parents had prepared us to be productive citizens, and we would all make our mark in some way. The banging of lockers between classes, the band at parades and football games, the sounds of friendly greetings and teenage chatter, the drones of teachers' lectures, and that wonderful public address system would go with us and remind us of those days. Surely, pink lemonade, color words, and star athletes would follow us forever.

Student council officers at West Tallahatchie High School:
Billy Gip Clark, Anne Hart Morrow, Jane Shaw, Bobo Catoe

Pink Bows, Permanents, and Porch Parties

There were some things that just happened without planning, without provocation, and without prelude. Life happened in the slow lane, and there was no reason to rush. If a passing vehicle created a wave of dust as it flew down the gravel road, it did not matter because we knew it would eventually settle until the next car or truck came along. Daily existence revolved around going to school, inventing some sort of gathering for socializing, making an identity statement, or preparing for those things by shopping or by obtaining beauty regardless of the sacrifice. Through all the years, the porch was the hub of our activity, and it made for a unique setting for holidays or celebrations or morning meditations.

My formative years were rather unique, and I have become convinced that it had to do with having three adults in the house and with being so remotely situated in the country without television. It did not hinder us, though, from making our own statements or creating our own niche in rather unique fashions.

As a preschooler, I was bald. There was not one string of hair upon my slick head, and Mother grew quite weary of defending my gender, so she practiced the habit of making pink bows and attaching them to my scalp with scotch tape. Research has yet to determine if there are long-term effects of scotch tape attached to a toddler's bald head. Some scientist in years to come may make a startling discovery that will explain any and all actions of one Hitt Spur resident.

I did not have hair until I started to school, and even then, it was quite thin and fine. Most of the girls in my class had bangs, which I thought was quite the thing, so I came home from school one day (probably the day I moved from buzzards to bluebirds), found Mother's pinking shears and proceeded to adopt the latest look with bangs. The pinking shears added quite a different slant to the idea, though, and Mother had to put me in the car and take me to Miss Eunice's beauty parlor to straighten out—as best she could—the zigzag cut above my eyes. Miss Eunice did not usually do emergencies, but in my case she made an exception. There was not a lot she could do, but she made a valiant effort to restore some style. It was not until the second grade that the effects of my attempt at creating bangs disappeared.

As soon as there was a little more hair to deal with, Mother decided that I should have a permanent, and she loaded me up in the car and took me to Greenwood to Billye Parkinson's Beauty Shop, where I spent almost a weekend getting curls in my thin, baby-fine hair. (Billye and Mother had been classmates at Vaiden High School.) The age of the Toni permanent was torture personified. The smell of that acrid permanent will be forever etched into my sense of smell, and the misery of those permanent rods pulling my sensitive scalp was just a legal form of torture. Because my locks did not "hold" the curl for longer than about two months, the procedure was repeated in hopes that at some point a slight resemblance to Shirley Temple would take place.

Shirley Temple, child movie star of the '50s, is to blame for that ordeal of the permanent because every mother aspired for her daughter to have those adorable curls like Shirley, who danced and sang her way "On the Good Ship Lollipop" into America's heart. But, alas, Shirley Temple needed not fear for any competition from me, because the very few strands of hair I did have were quite rebellious toward the Toni permanent.

However, there were some redeeming points for the hair-curling experience, and those were Billye's three daughters, Sandra, Sue, and Sallye. Sandra was a year older than I, Sue was my age, and Sallye was a year younger, so it was like being with triplets. I would get to spend the night, and we would have great fun fixing hair and talking about boys. They had a room with three beds, which their father, George, called "the barracks," and I thought that was too cool. Being in the city of Greenwood was an experience for a country girl. Things were so different. People only associated with their own classmates, whereas in Tallahatchie County everybody was part of any event, no matter what grade they were in.

We would take turns, and the Parkinson girls would come to Hitt Spur for dances at the community house and to experience life in the country. Uncle Billy would ride them around in his Thunderbird for a special thrill. Birthday parties were events for everyone, and the more that came, the merrier. We never got too old for a grand occasion to celebrate the passing of another year. Mother would pull out all the stops for birthdays, and one very special one was a dress up party when all the little girls showed up in their mothers' fine dresses, hats, and gloves. The cake was in the shape of a lady's brimmed hat with pink icing, and we had to use the good china and silver. We really thought we had "arrived," and the Parkinson girls were on hand to help celebrate. Jane Shaw came to the party, and I was so glad to see her that I said to Sallye, "Hot dig, Jane's here." Forever after, she was known by the girls as *Jane Hot Dig*.

Birthday parties were not the only things we shared. There were the elaborate recitals Mrs. Prosser engineered for her piano and organ students. Sue took organ while Sallye and Sandra concentrated on the piano. Mrs. Prosser insisted that Sue and I have our senior organ recital at Greenwood and at Webb, and, not wanting to upset her, we did just that. I am not sure who was more pleased when those ordeals were over, Mrs. Prosser or us. I really think she was holding her breath the whole time—afraid that we might launch into a rock and roll tune instead of the classical pieces she had insisted we perform. We were known to have somewhat of an independent streak at times, but we chose to adhere to the rules for this event.

Sallye, Sue, and Sandra thought it was fun that I had a pink room all to myself, two brothers, plus another adult in the house. The ninety-foot-long porch was also a fascination as well. That porch was the setting for all kinds of events from birthday parties to holiday celebrations and prenuptial gatherings. It was also where I opened my first and last barber shop. I decided one day that I could cut hair as well as Mr. Berry and persuaded Will to let me practice on him. I got the scissors off Mother's sewing machine and proceeded to shape Will into the latest fashion. When he took a look in the mirror, he ran screaming off the porch to seek solace under a far tree, where not even his black rubber boots could console him. Mother came out onto the porch walking very fast with the butter paddle, and my barbershop was closed permanently.

The porch was part of who we were because we spent so much time there. Drinking coffee in the early mornings and listening to the sounds of the morning as the day woke itself up offered a time to just sit and enjoy the quiet. Coffee and the porch are synonymous, for it seems like we drank a lot of coffee out there. In the middle of the afternoon we had coffee and cake, and, especially on Sunday afternoons, the Houstons and Bradshaws would find their way to the front porch. Coffee and cake would be served then in the fine china with the Old Master silver; there was no allowance for a paper plate or a plastic fork. At other times, we shelled mountains of peas and butterbeans out there and felt very safe from the snakes we knew were lurking out in the yard. We were positive snakes could not climb the five steps and wiggle through the screen door, but we kept one eye peeled for any reptile intruders, just in case.

The Fourth of July brought practically the whole county to the porch for a celebration of our nation's independence. Grilled hamburgers, chicken, and hot dogs, along with fabulous peach ice cream that did not have too many calories—but then, who was counting—satisfied our hunger after a rousing game of horseshoes, croquet, or a quick softball match pitting the adults against the children. The whirring of the ice-cream freezer was drowned out by the cheers and jeers of those involved in the various activities.

To make the peach ice cream, you needed a quart of mashed ripe peaches, with sugar to taste, one quart of half and half cream, one quart of whole milk. Mix, and then pour it all in the ice-cream freezer and wait for the magic to happen.

The porch also served as an alarm to signal our arrival after a date because there was no way to walk the ninety feet and not make noise. To this day, I am convinced the night air magnified our steps. Curfews were strictly enforced, and we only had to miss once to know that we did not want to repeat the consequences. Sweeping that porch was hard enough when it was our turn, but when it was meted out as punishment, those ninety feet tripled.

Shirley Temple's influence—along with the Toni permanent—has dissipated over the years, and the pinking shears with their jagged edges have been retired to some drawer unknown, while pink bows with the long-term effect of scotch tape on skin are still the subject of intense research. Vehicles still create clouds of dust as they pass through Hitt Spur, and the echoes of parties and friends gathering permeate the quiet mornings and peaceful afternoons. The rocking chairs are stilled now, and beauty continues to be elusive, but the friendships and connections formed and enriched at Hitt Spur are bonds that will never be broken.

Sue Parkinson, Sallye Parkinson, Anne Hart
Morrow, Robert Morrow, Sandra Parkinson

Stage Planks, RC Colas, and the Rainbow's End

When Robert, Will, and I learned to ride our bikes, the yard could no longer contain us, and the gravel road beckoned us to new worlds like *the* store operated by Pop Wilson. It was at the end of the road about three-fourths of a mile, and was a huge, green, wooden building that was amazing because it had an apartment in the back where Mr. Wilson lived. The cavernous wood building contained anything and everything a heart could desire, including the best stage planks (pink icing on a gingerbread slab), and the coldest RC Colas. For a dime, those delightful sweets could be ours and would satisfy our sweet tooth for a while. Those RC Colas would chase the stage planks on down, and our thirst would be quenched. Ah, what treasures awaited us at the end of that gravel road.

Sometimes on hot summer days, Dora Sue and I would navigate the cotton fields from her house to the store to get a banana popsicle. We traveled through the field so often that we formed a path through the cotton plants. Other times, we would ride our bicycles and get many skinned knees and elbows from wrecks on the gravel road, but that did not stop us from our quest to reach *the* store. Pop was always glad to see us and was ready to provide some sort of refreshment to revive us after our trek in the scorching Delta sun. He kept a tab if we had forgotten our nickels. When drinks went from a nickel to six cents, Dora Sue and I were livid, and we threatened to stop drinking altogether, but that was short lived. Pop just added another penny to our bill.

Pop was tall, bald-headed, and thin, with a gentle manner and quiet voice. He enjoyed talking to his customers and swapping fish stories. He would lean over the counter and ask us, "What's going on in the small world today?" which made us a little irritated because we thought we were grown, but we shrugged it off as the goings-on of an old man. We didn't want to get him too disturbed because if he got mad, his face and head would turn red. Instead, we would turn our attention to our RC Colas, sit on the steps of the store, and pour peanuts into our drinks while we watched Pop pump gas for twenty-five cents a gallon for a customer. There was always something to entertain us at *the* store. If Pop wasn't dispensing gasoline, he was spouting forth wisdom about anything and everything. We were a captive audience, spellbound by the stories he could spin.

Pop didn't really have scheduled hours of operation; since he lived there, he could stay open as long as a customer was around. In the summer, he was open for the hoe hands, who had piled onto the back of a pickup truck to travel to the fields at dawn, and he awaited them at the last glimmer of twilight when they were returning home. They were ready for some food and drink after a long day of chopping weeds in the cotton fields that stretched endlessly. During harvest season, he seemed to be open twenty-four hours a day, seven days a week for those picking the white bolls of cotton they had rescued from the weeds. He didn't seem to mind, though. He probably took a nap in one of those big rocking chairs scattered about in the store when he got tired. He would say, "I gotta make hay while the sun shines," and while we didn't see any hay, we knew the sun was shining. Our *small world* didn't comprehend everything.

The days seemed to roll along endlessly, and our joy at escaping from the yard knew no bounds. We couldn't wait to get our barefooted, sweat-beaded selves to *the* store for our daily ration of RC Colas, stage planks, and maybe a popsicle or some peanuts if we were rich. Little did we know that those days were coming to a screeching halt.

One night, Pop was sleeping soundly when he was awakened by a strange noise. An intruder had entered the store with a gun, demanding the money from Pop's ancient cash register. There wasn't much money, and the robber took his anger out on Pop with a whack to his head. Pop regained consciousness and called the law. Someone took him to Dr. Lacey, who stitched him up and told him to take some aspirin, but Pop locked the doors, packed up, and left. Pop said he was too old to be scared for his life, and we didn't blame him.

Maudie Clay immortalized *the* store in her book, *Delta Land*, but that picture was taken years after Pop had gone, and the popsicles, stage planks, and cold RC Colas had disappeared. For just a little while, though, we could journey through the cotton fields or down the gravel road to what seemed like the pot of gold at the end of the rainbow with our very own wizard, Pop Wilson, dispensing stories and wonderful refreshments in a magic land. Pop, and the store with its gigantic inside kept cool by the open doors and extremely high ceilings, had been part of our small world. They had both captivated and enchanted us, and our fascination was unceasing. However, those days could not last, for the robber was never captured; Pop never returned, and *the* store was gone forever.

The Green Bomb and the *store*

The Final Farewell

Life had its share of rituals and celebrations, and death imitated it, so a person's last farewell was symbolic of his life's journey. The marking of a person's passing to the next life meant observing certain customs. Children were shielded from the harsh realities of life's ending until they were deemed old enough to handle the finality of a person's existence on the earth. Customs were observed religiously and without fail, and there are some funerals, as there are individuals, that forever remain embedded in our recollections.

One custom that has become obscured with time is that the deceased was taken to the home to be viewed by friends and family, but it forever marked that room as the spot where Aunt so-and-so or Miss so-and-so had lain. Family and friends were called upon to sit up with the body all night. When Aunt Lallie died, her body was taken back to the house on Summit Street. I was probably eight or nine at the time, and I was haunted by the fear that she might get out of the casket and walk around. I do not remember if anyone stayed up with the body or not. I, for one, did not sleep a wink that night, so I might as well have stayed up with the body. I could never walk in that dining room without picturing her in the casket and am glad that custom has not continued.

Funerals were a time of seeing friends and relatives, and of reminiscing about times gone by. Funerals were a social event. Paying one's respects was the thing to do, no matter if the deceased was a slight acquaintance or a close relative or friend. Funerals were "must attend" events. Mother's friends always talked about how many cars were behind a person's hearse, and they always feared that there would not be many behind theirs.

Even though funerals were sad occasions, some were marked with unique circumstances making them events to remember and reminisce about for generations. Take the lady from Tutwiler who died after traveling around the country on a train for years. She was quite a flamboyant character and believed in living life to the fullest. She married several times and then had a few gentlemen friends. When it came time for her "service," all the husbands and gentlemen friends showed up. The ushers were not sure where to seat them all, and at last the funeral home director made them all honorary pallbearers so they sat in a place of honor without having the distinction of sitting in the "family" pews.

Then there was the very hot August day when the hearse carrying the deceased to the cemetery broke down on the side of the road. The procession had to wait for another hearse to be sent from Clarksdale, which was twenty-five miles away. Those in the procession began to drop like flies with the intense summer heat bearing down. The flowers in the funeral sprays began to wither, and the day did not get any better when the spouse and the driver of the hearse almost got into a fistfight. There, on the side of the road between Webb and Sumner, was a scene no one could have ever imagined. "Only in Tallahatchie County," folks would say. People used to remark that the deceased would be late for his own funeral, and their predictions came true—at least to the cemetery.

Perhaps the stalling of the hearse on an August day was not the most notable occurrence. One of the more memorable funerals happened at Hitt Chapel when the casket was being lowered into the ground. The funeral home had cut some corners in the burial outfit and had not clothed the deceased from the waist down. When the pallbearers were lowering the casket into the ground, the ropes broke, breaking the casket into splinters and spilling the deceased into full view. The funeral had to be delayed while the funeral director returned to Tutwiler for another casket and garments. Under the watchful eyes of the family, the director made sure the deceased was covered. The funeral home director made sure the ropes were secure, and the ushers revived everyone to end that service.

Another custom associated with death and dying is that of taking food to the family of the deceased. Everyone in the community would bring food, so there was an abundance of good morsels to devour and assuage our grief. Because the custom of visitation usually happened at the church or at the home where the body lay in state, the food was a source of comfort and convenience for the relatives and friends who gathered to support one another in a sad time. The ladies of the community always had a casserole of some description in the freezer for just such an occasion, and for those who did not, the first notice of the death sent some into their kitchen to whip up the most delicious of cakes. There was some stiff competition, too, in who would take the best "dish," and the recipes were carefully guarded so as to maintain secrecy regarding ingredients and preparation. One newcomer to the community mistakenly asked for the recipe to a masterpiece coconut cake and was told, "Honey, if I tell you,

I'll have to kill you." Food was never lacking, and it buffered the awkwardness of the loved one's passing. It somehow filled the void for a brief moment.

People used to talk about death coming in threes, and sure enough it does seem to be true. Small communities note the passing of friends and loved ones because everyone knows everyone else, and so each death is marked by phone calls and prayer chains and taking food to the family. Notice in your own circumstances whether or not the Grim Reaper has taken his victims in sets of three. No one can explain why this happens; it just does.

The custom of sending funeral sprays was exercised frequently. Uncle Billy told the story of going to the florist shop in Winona to purchase some flowers for a funeral, and there in the window was a funeral spray in the shape of a telephone. Across the phone was the phrase "Jesus called." We were never sure whom Jesus called, but we all hoped he got the right number.

At least the tradition of going to funerals has continued in the Delta, even with the advent of busy schedules and work. The ritual of paying respects to the departed's family is expected and is the right thing to do. Even now in the South, when a funeral procession is approaching on the highway, people still practice the custom of pulling off the road until the main part of the funeral procession has passed. It is a way to acknowledge a loved one's passing and the loss of someone dear in the lives of those riding in those cars.

I have come to believe that it is also an unconscious acknowledgement of our own mortality and the hope that whoever meets our procession on the road will take a few moments out of a busy schedule to stop and pay respects to our brief existence on this planet. Perhaps, too, they will wonder what kind of people we were, what we did, or speculate about the cause of our demise.

Afterword

Memories come and go, revealing times, things, people, and places, in no particular order or significance. Like the mists hovering over the fields in the early morning hours before the sun lifts above the horizon to mark another day, the memories linger for moments, obscuring portions of reality, and then they vanish, only to reappear again when time and circumstances permit.

Years pass and memories accumulate, and I am reminded more and more that the present is enriched by the past. We live in a time that is fast paced and moving faster. But there is inherent in the human being a desire to know what was before, to reflect on who we are and how we got here. Our existence is marked by turning points forming us in ways that we might not understand at the moment; looking back may be a clear view, or it might be clouded by vague memories.

I look out each morning as I walk along rice fields and see that rice and soybeans have taken the place of the once king, cotton. Agriculture is still the major economy of the area, but instead of forty families with forty mules, there might be four people to run a farm. I think about a lot of things as I take that ritual walk, and the thing that keeps going through my mind is that the more things change, the more they stay the same. It is true. The Delta has seen a lot of change in the last fifty years, but the boundaries are still there, hidden, under the surface, reminding us of where we are and who we have been. The memories are fleeting, chased by the realities of the harsh morning sun making its way over the horizon. A new day dawns, and the old one slips into memory. People, places, events become blurred as the years progress, but always there are the connections—friendships, family, customs—that are part of us and define us in unique, timeless ways.

Acknowledgements

This book could not have been possible without the support, encouragement, and contributions of friends and family. For all who conjured up memories and shared them, I am forever grateful. I appreciate those whose shared photographs helped to add a more realistic dimension to this work.

A special thanks goes to Kaye Rendfrey, who gave me an opportunity to put pen to paper several years ago. Then, along the way, she gave me gentle nudges of encouragement. She provided me with opportunities to stretch my imagination and see what I could accomplish even before this book was an idea.

The Clark family lived *down the gravel road* and was an integral part of my life. Dora Sue, Billy Gip, and Hugh Gregory were all a year ahead of Robert, Will, and me. They were the younger children of Vorena and Gip Clark, who had three older children who were almost a separate family. Clara, Mary Ruth, and Lacey Booth rounded out the family and served as mentors to the younger ones. I cannot imagine growing up without them.

The Shaw family was my "town family" and provided a place to spend the night on many occasions when school activities would have placed me on the gravel road at night by myself. Jane, James Arnette, and Mr. and Mrs. Shaw were part of the village it took to raise me.

Duff Dorough designed the cover, and his talents are unparalleled.

Lastly, this book could not have been possible without the editorial skills of Gary Walker, whose patience and encouragement have been immeasurable.